Museum Development in China

Museum Development in China

Understanding the Building Boom

Edited by Gail Dexter Lord, Guan Qiang,
An Laishun, and Javier Jimenez

Editorial Coordinators Ai Jingfang and Rebecca Catching

ROWMAN & LITTLEFIELD
Lanham • Boulder • New York • London

Published by Rowman & Littlefield
An imprint of The Rowman & Littlefield Publishing Group, Inc.
4501 Forbes Boulevard, Suite 200, Lanham, Maryland 20706
www.rowman.com

6 Tinworth Street, London SE11 5AL, United Kingdom

British Library Cataloguing in Publication Information Available

Library of Congress Cataloging-in-Publication Data

Names: Lord, Gail Dexter, 1946– editor.
Title: Museum development in China : understanding the building boom / edited by Gail Dexter Lord, Guan Qiang, An Laishun, and Javier Jimenez.
Description: Lanham : Rowman & Littlefield, 2019. | Includes bibliographical references and index.
Identifiers: LCCN 2019005458 (print) | LCCN 2019009134 (ebook) | ISBN 9781538109984 (electronic) | ISBN 9781538109977 (cloth : alk. paper)
Subjects: LCSH: Museums—China—History—21st century. | Museums—China—Case studies.
Classification: LCC AM72.A2 (ebook) | LCC AM72.A2 M87 2019 (print) | DDC 069.0951/0905—dc23
LC record available at https://lccn.loc.gov/2019005458

CONTENTS

LIST OF FIGURES

ACKNOWLEDGMENTS

This book would not have been possible without the generosity of all those who took time from their regular work to collaborate across the time zones of China, Europe, the United States, and Canada to present a portrait of the remarkable development of Chinese museums. Our thanks go also to the curators, architects, designers, planners, cultural managers, and funders whose commitment to building and sustaining museums has resulted in their growth worldwide and especially in China.

This book is the culmination of two consecutive memoranda of understanding (2011–2018) between the Chinese Museums Association (CMA) and Lord Cultural Resources, the Canadian-based international cultural planning firm. The goal of the MOUs was to enhance the museum sector in China through educational initiatives that brought international museologists together with Chinese museum leaders and enthusiastic new members of the field. We thank all those participants for their lively discussions, which generated many of the ideas that form the core of this book.

It was at one of these education sessions that Barry Lord (1939–2017) co-founder of Lord Cultural Resources suggested the idea of this book to the President of the CMA. Inquisitive about the rapid development of Chinese museums, he felt others would likewise be enthusiastic to learn more about this phenomenon. Barry's love of museums suffuses this volume and our work.

We are grateful to our colleagues from Beijing Lord International Cultural Development Co., Ltd. & Beijing Lord Times Cultural Industry Development Co., Ltd., Guan Jian, and Song Rufen, as well as to Wei Hongquan, for their professional contribution and financial support for the book. An international project of this magnitude would not have been possible without their aid.

Readers will notice that this is an intercultural book in which 16 chapters originated in Chinese and 10 originated in English. Coordinating and editing the content required fluency not only in translation and retranslation between Chinese and English and back again, but also deep understanding of museums and the language we use to explain them. Fortunately for all of us, our two editorial coordinators, Ai Jingfang, vice secretary general of the CMA, and Rebecca Catching, an independent Canadian curator who lived and worked in the Chinese museum sector for many years, were able to create that miracle together. Ai Jingfang took the lead in liaising with the Chinese authors and soliciting their manuscripts, editing and facilitating their translation from Chinese to English. Rebecca worked with the translated texts to shape them into seamless chapters that would be more easily understood by Western audiences. There was also a great deal of organizational work, including innumerable hours collecting copyright permissions and liaising with authors.

Deep appreciation to all our authors who made original contributions that took the book in new and interesting directions and enhanced its academic stature. We thank them for their adaptability and persistence as we tried to shape the book into something both comprehensive and readable. Many of our authors deserve extra thanks for their efforts to procure images for us that help to illustrate both specific topics and the robust variety of architectural forms that characterize China's museum landscape.

With so many authors and so much information, the support staff of the Chinese Museums Association and Lord Cultural Resources worked tirelessly to pull the various pieces together. We would like to express our sincere gratitude to Mira Ovanin for her management of the project and numerous useful insights since the outset, to Rebecca Frerotte, who assembled the bibliography and coordinated the submission to the publisher, and to Michelle Selmen, who designed the cover and prepared the manuscript for publication. Luo Man, professor at Hunan University, acted as the main translator of Chinese articles from their original language to English, and Liu Young worked procuring images from various sources and databases, and assisted with translation.

Finally, these acknowledgments would not be complete without a heartfelt thanks to Charles Harmon of Rowman & Littlefield for his continuing encouragement and support of our work throughout many successful collaborations, which has allowed us and our readers to deepen our understanding of these wildly variable, vital, and constantly evolving institutions that are museums.

The Editors
January 2019

PREFACE

The Chinese Museum Boom in Broad Strokes

Guan Qiang

China's rapid economic and social development over the last four decades—often regarded as a miracle by many people—has greatly benefited the museum sector.

In the past eight years, we have seen the number of museums increase by 200 a year to reach a total of 5,136 museums nationwide. This number represents a 230-fold increase since 1949. The next five years will continue to see new growth in the construction of "large" museums—defined as museums over 20,000 square meters—and "super large" museums (50,000 square meters), but the trend going forward is to support more modest infrastructure projects.

There is a general consensus that one or several successful museums in a city can play a significant role in building both the city's soft power and public cultural life. And that's why not only state actors and institutions, but also the private sector have played strong roles in leading and guiding this boom. Private museums have also seen vigorous growth and development. In the eyes of the general public, the image of traditional museums has also changed. Today's museums do not espouse the elitist attitude of the past, with no connection to everyday people; rather they are more open, inclusive, and dynamic. Museums in China are public cultural and educational institutions that attempt to serve the comprehensive needs of the public. In 2017, there were 970 million museum visits. To some extent, visiting museums is becoming a habit for a cross section of the population, not merely reserved for wealthy or intellectual urbanites. 4.6 percent of the Chinese household's consumption expenditure is on average now spent on cultural products, and despite the boom in physical building, the visitor numbers seem to be outpacing the numbers of museums, showing a growing demand for museum experiences.

At the same time, museums in China are also gaining ground internationally. China is not only sharing its excellent collections with other nations, but it has also hosted many exhibitions of international artworks and artifacts. This has not only helped create an awareness of the evolution of ancient China but also helped foster a greater understanding of the achievements of other nations. With frequent collaborations with world-famous institutions, international forums, and museum conferences hosted in China, and frequent exchanges of Chinese professionals who travel abroad for training, we can expect deeper and more meaningful dialogue in the future—a dialogue of which this book is a part.

With such rapid museum growth, it is tempting to wonder if the current boom is a temporary phenomenon or a long-term trend with global significance. To answer this question, we need to consider a variety of factors. It is self-evident that part of this boom is due to the country's rapid economic development, which has made China the world's second-largest economy. The economic growth has resulted in an improvement in living standards and education. The nation and its cities have moved beyond the focus on manufacturing and now understand the value of the knowledge economy and creative industries. Over the last decade, the creative industries have seen 60-fold growth, which represented 4.6 percent of GDP in

2015, but in cities such as Beijing, which has a high concentration of cultural industries, represented 12 percent of municipal GDP.

Museums have already become an important part of China's overall development strategy—a fact that makes it seem likely that this boom is not a temporary phenomenon. Government policy has stressed the educational function of museums but at the same time emphasized that museums need to embrace a more public-facing attitude. This involves a reorientation of the function of museums that focuses on how to *animate* the artifacts, ancient texts, and heritage sites. While previously the primary focus was on collecting, studying, and preserving artifacts, today's museums are also concerned with how to "serve society, promote development, and improve the livelihood of the people."

Yet at the same time, on the road ahead lie a number of challenges, including management systems, the balance between the number of museums and the quality of content, talent development, and the creation of uniqueness and diversity in the museum ecosystem. With big plans on the horizon for museum districts in Shanghai, Shenzhen, and a north branch of the Palace Museum, the future of Chinese museums is hotly anticipated. This book can be viewed as a review and summary of the challenges and successes, providing us with projections and possible future visions of China's museum boom.

INTRODUCTION

Understanding China's Museum Building Boom

Gail Lord

Some Chinese scholars trace the origin of museums in their country to 478 BCE—that is the year after the death of Confucius.[1] A special temple in his former residence displayed his carriage, clothes, and appliances so people could pay respect and study how to conduct rituals and ceremonies.

Display for purposes of respecting authority and educating people are age-old motivators for the creation of museums, and there are many such museums among the approximately 50,000 to 80,000[2] in the world today. However, the global growth of museums in the 21st century has broadened the scope of museums, including many new types of museums—and nowhere more so than in China.

The growth of the number and scale of Chinese museums in the 21st century, from about 1,400 at the turn of the century to over 5,000 to date, reflects the government's Museum Development Plan for 2011–2020 to open one museum per 250,000 inhabitants, with the goal of attracting one billion visitors at the end of the decade. There are already 970 million museum visitors in China—which is about the same number as in the United States, a much smaller population.

Despite the tremendous growth over the last 40 years, China is still behind other countries when comparing the number of museums per number of inhabitants: 1 museum for every 278,431[3] Chinese residents, while the United Kingdom has 1 museum for every 26,259[4] inhabitants, and the United States 1 for every 9,346.[5] This suggests that the need for museums in China will grow in the years to come.

It is not just the numbers but the speed of development of Chinese museums that takes our breath away—with nearly one new museum per day being opened or expanded in this huge country.

What are the motivations for the rapid development of museums in China? How is the public responding? Who pays for these museums and how? What has been the impact of China's urbanization? How do Chinese museums balance education, scientific research, social cohesion, cultural diplomacy, and tourism both internal and external? These are issues that continue to be discussed and debated among Western museum professionals in the context of our 200-year history of modern museology. How are these debates evolving in China, which has its own history of museology over that same period from colonialism to communism and from isolation to opening up to the world?

This book explores these issues while introducing English-language readers to a sample of the new Chinese museums in case studies and photographs. To accomplish this goal, we have partnered with the Chinese Museums Association (CMA), who engaged leading Chinese museologists, museum directors, academics, and architects to provide chapters and case studies on the history of museums in China; on evolving national museum policies, museum exhibitions, and cultural diplomacy; on the role of private museums; and on the impact of museums on society. We reached out to Western contributors from such diverse fields as architecture, urban planning, curatorial practice, and museum planning to contribute essays on Chinese museums in the exploding urban environment,

Figure 1 The former residence of Confucius at Qufu in Shandong is said to be the first "museum" in China. After the death of Confucius in 478 BCE, his clothes, carriage, and other implements were put on display. *Photography: Michael Gunther*

in place-making, the creative economy, contemporary expression, and public engagement.

The four parts of this book build our knowledge of the roles of China's museums through social and political changes, the systems of governance, the complex relationships between private and public sectors, and many levels of government.

Part 1 places the current building boom in context. Dr. An Laishun provides an overview of the story of Chinese museology. Coeditor Javier Jimenez and I identify two comparable museum building booms in the global north and west and propose some causes—urbanization in particular— that can be seen at work in China today. Professors Song Xiangguang and Duan Yong contribute brief histories of Chinese museums. Sofia Ballo and Yu Zhang navigate the complex territories of evolving museum policy, practice, and funding, connecting them to social change and cultural

diplomacy. Han Young analyzes the policies that balance preservation and public access.

Part 2 addresses how China's rapid urbanization has fueled the museum building boom, framed it, formed it, and in some cases financed it. Doug Saunders, who is an expert on urbanization and migration, writes about the specific ways that Chinese cities grow and how real estate development impacts new museums throughout the country. Gao Peng provides a lively example of a new museum "born," as he says, from the real estate industry in Beijing. Urban planner Phil Enquist shares his experience working with many new Chinese cities as they develop from a laser focus on densification to embrace a sense of place through culture, especially museums and parks. He Jingtang explains why symbolic architecture has become the hallmark of China's newest museums and how his team at the South China University of Technology has worked with the "genius loci" of place and community to design museums over the past decade. Rebecca Catching describes how private art museums—many of them in urban mixed-use developments—are building bridges between contemporary art and local residents.

China's opening up to the world in the 1980s was prefigured in the 1970s with the memorable 16-nation tour of "Unearthed Cultural Relics from the People's Republic of China." Part 3 analyzes how Chinese exhibitions are tools for cultural diplomacy (Zhou Ming) and key elements of soft power (An Laishun). Canadian curator Chen Shen shares his experience and advice on conducting international exhibition exchange. Tomislav Sola sees new forms of public engagement emerging from China's global cultural activities. Tian Kai explains how opening up to Western influence has profoundly changed Chinese museum philosophy. Tim Reeve contributes an insightful chapter on the V&A partnership with the Design Society in Shenzhen.

The six case studies in Part 4 provide perspectives on the diversity of innovative approaches in the sector. Yang Zhigang describes the impact of a British Museum "blockbuster" on management; Wei Jun explains how China's museums are harnessing technology; Shan Jixiang and Chen Ruijin explain what it means to be visitor-centered at the Palace and Suzhou Museums respectively, while Jian Guan reflects on the popularity of natural history museums. Our closing case study by architect Zhu Pei inspires with the relevance and beauty of the Imperial Kiln Museum and its centuries-old kilns in contemporary China.

This book is an international collaboration to discover how much East and West can learn from each other about museum roles, our publics, how we preserve, what we conserve, and our future sustainability—even as we marvel at the accomplishments of China's museum building boom. All of us working with and in the ever-changing museum sector are (as evoked so well in this Chinese expression) "feeling the stones as we cross the river."

CHINA'S MUSEUM BOOM IN CONTEXT

2 The Suzhou Museum (1960, 2006), designed by architect I. M. Pei.
Photography: Zhangzhugang

1

LIVELY PLACES THROBBING WITH LIFE

An Laishun

As lively places throbbing with life, today's museums stand in sharp contrast to the desolate, dark, and dusty institutions of 30 years ago. Part of this change has, of course, been driven by the visitor. The viewing public, who 30 years ago had few opportunities to even travel to different cities within their own province, and now travel all over China and around the world, and their tastes have changed accordingly. Along with China's increasing economic power comes a new demand for diverse cultural products. It's a story that very much reflects the stories of other countries as they transitioned into developed economies. But what is unique about China's situation is that while Western governments are beginning to retreat from their role as cultural investors, the Chinese government has increased its investment in cultural heritage from 3.76 billion RMB in 2006 to 25.85 billion RMB in 2013—a sixfold increase. China's museum boom has also seen other important drivers, such as the basic need for capacity building. Like many other countries in the developing world, China has relatively few institutions in comparison to its population. In the 1980s, during the "Reform and Opening-Up" ushered in by Deng Xiaoping, China had as few as 349 museums with a population of 963 million. But rising economic prosperity signaled a change in government policy. While the government had previously measured its progress based on pure economic growth, it began to seek a balance between the economy and regional and cultural indicators—a new understanding from local government officials of the subtle relationship between GDP and the value of soft power.

It was clear that museums were to play an important role in the national cultural ecology, but at the same time, this rapid expansion brought with it expected growing pains. The quality of institutions was not always matched with the speed of their construction, and museums lacked both adequate systems and mechanisms. Some museums,

though outdated and ossified (in terms of their hardware and systems), opted to avoid the risks and complications involved in changing their management approach—a decision that left them floundering in a state of untapped potential. Some newly established museums suffered from inadequate collections and a singular and limiting collections policy. Today the contradiction between the lack of collections and the lack of funds *required to build* collections is coming out in stark relief. Other museums face the challenges of high overheads—with their vast and spacious architecture consuming all of their revenues in the form of utility bills.

Beyond the issue of hardware, staffing is still a major challenge for many institutions, with positions sitting vacant for long periods of time due to the lack of qualified applicants. This bottleneck in professional training and development and the lack of supportive policies leaves many museums operating just below their potential, unable to go that last mile to success.

Though the education sector has seen phenomenal growth with 47 colleges and universities offering museum-related courses and degree programs—six times that of ten years ago—the curriculum currently does not address the diversity of museum types and the structural contradictions between the curriculum and the practical needs of the museum. One of the deep-seated reasons for this problem is the lack of recognition of museology in the Chinese academic system—which is viewed as a lesser discipline of sorts.

While educational offerings scramble to catch up with the industry, there is a much bigger issue looming on the horizon—the question of the continued availability and sustainability of government resources—a topic that

Figure 3 The façade of the Ningbo Museum (2008) is composed of fragments of the past—terra cotta roof tiles and old bricks from the surrounding neighborhoods. Looking closely, viewers can even find the date and name of the manufacturer of the bricks. *Photography: Chao Zhen. Photo courtesy: Chinese Museums Association Architecture and Technology Committee, China Archive of Museum Architecture, and the Nanjing Museum*

many museum professionals would prefer to leave untouched. While it is too early to conclude that an economic downturn would affect the development of museums, it is possible that governments may only sustain this huge investment for a certain period of time in order to allow the museum system to take root. It is unrealistic to anticipate a steady, continuous flow of investment into museum coffers. Regrettably, it seems that most museums in China are not poised to meet this challenge.

We can, however, take hope in the fact that changes in governance structures will help usher in more contemporary management practices to help museums prepare for this formidable obstacle. Since 2011, more and more institutions, all across the country, are eagerly forming boards of trustees—something rarely seen in China in the past—to improve the professionalism of governance. Today, most state-owned museums and 75 percent of private museums at the city and provincial level have a board of trustees in place. The function of these boards varies. In some institutions, the board acts as a coordinator; in others, it takes on a consultant role or is involved in policy

making. In many cases, the board plays an instructive role in securing a democratic approach in the creation of policy—safeguarding the general public's rights to be involved in the management of public affairs.

On the topic of inclusivity, Chinese museums have also made great strides in terms of outreach with the full implementation of the free-admissions policy. The policy was supported by government subsidies of 15 billion RMB in total over five years.

Implemented in 2008, by 2017, the policy saw over 4,262 museums of various types offering free-admission tickets to the general public in China, roughly 87.1 percent of all museums. In response to this stimulus we have seen the audience of each museum grow by over 50 percent, attracting migrant laborers, urban low-income workers, and other groups who previously experienced barriers to entry.

Chinese museums are also trying to extend their reach in a virtual sense with a recent push toward digitalization. The First National Survey of Movable Cultural Heritage was conducted from 2012 to 2017—a mammoth task whereby over 64 million collection items were either filed or refiled digitally. The survey not only helped to inventory the collections of public museums but also standardized the descriptions of these objects, to pave the way for the future sharing of this information with the public.

Private museums, which were previously left to more-or-less fend for themselves, have seen their fortunes improve due to a change in government attitudes since 2010. This involved new regulations and policies to encourage, support, guide, and regulate the development of private museums toward healthy and sustainable growth. In 2010, eight ministries including the National Cultural Heritage Administration released a policy to support and encourage the private museums. This policy was the first of its kind, a sort of "trans-institutional peer support program," outlining 16 areas of concern and the enforcement and implementation of a series of regulations to help private museums to solve the "last mile" problem.

In the next five years, China will roll out several research and development projects dealing with pressing topics such as collecting intangible heritage and talent development—initiatives such as the Collection of Objects Reflecting Socio-Economic Change, the National Memory Project, the Golden Tripod Project for Professional Development, the Traditional Crafts and Artisans Project, and the National Movable Cultural Heritage Project. Therefore, through both public and private sector engagement, we can look forward to continued evolution and transformation of this robust and dynamic sector.

2

A GLOBAL PERSPECTIVE ON MUSEUM "BOOMS" AND GROWTH CYCLES

Javier Jimenez and Gail Lord

Change, In Context

Nobody knows exactly how many museums there are in the world today, mainly because there is no single definition of what a museum is. Different listings of museums tend to count different types of institutions, including or excluding categories such as zoos, historical societies, botanical gardens, and historical or cultural sites. Nevertheless, it is safe to say that the number of museums today is somewhere between 50,000 and 80,000,[1] two-thirds of them in the developed north and west of the globe.

While China has opened more museums in the last one and half decades than all other countries combined, it has not been the only country experiencing rapid museum growth. Almost 50 percent of today's museums were built in the last twenty years. Nations in the Middle East have become tourism destinations thanks to the opening of a dozen world-class museums where a decade or two ago there was only desert. The number of museums in the United States has doubled since the 1990s, from 17,500 to around 35,000,[2] and in the last five years alone, the U.S. museum sector has grown by an annual rate of 4.2 percent.

A "museum boom" is a period of time in which a much higher-than-average number of museums are created or expanded. At first glance, it seems counterintuitive that reflective institutions like museum institutions are products of boom cycles. Does this imply they will also experience "busts"? What can we learn from these cycles? How do they impact the public, and what are the best ways for the museum profession to respond to these phenomena? These questions are also what prompted this book.

Any museum boom correlates strongly to two factors: rapid economic development, and urbanization. Both factors lead to social transformations and deep changes in human values and ways of seeing the world. Museums, which are not only repositories of human knowledge but also creators of meaning, undergo fundamental change during these boom periods. There are no museum booms during times of recession or economic stagnation. Culture competes for resources with other more primary needs such as labor, education, or health, and when resources are scarce, museums lose ground against other priorities. Very few museums were built during the post–world war years in Europe, in the last decades of the communist era in the USSR, or since the Gulf War of 1990–1991 in the countries along the Fertile Crescent (Iran, Syria, Iraq, Jordan).

The rate of urbanization is an indicator of the transformation of society from agricultural and industrial to a knowledge economy. The majority of museums are in urban settings, where the density of population is high and heavy investment in infrastructure and real estate is undertaken. Since the burst of industrialization in the 19th century, which favored the manufacturing and service economy over agriculture, populations have migrated from the countryside looking for new opportunities in the urban environment. China joined in this transition later than other countries: the growth of cities was held back by a policy of "rustication" or deurbanization from 1963 to 1978 when young people and families were sent "down to the villages" and "up into the mountains"—which explains why museums did not boom during that time. It is not until the Reform and Opening-Up in the 1980s that China's cities were encouraged to grow. This re-urbanization laid the groundwork for museum growth.

Not coincidentally, countries with the highest urban population rates are the ones with the lowest museum-to-residents ratio—which is on average less than 50,000 inhabitants per museum in Europe and North America—far exceeding the Chinese ratio of one museum for every 278,431 residents.[3] Economic and urbanization statistics suggest that there is still space for more museum growth in China: urban population in China represents 53 percent, still below most developed countries, which are in the 80 percent range.[4]

The First Museum Boom: 1780–1900

Museums have existed for centuries as collections of valued objects. The modern concept of a museum as a public space for learning and enjoyment arises also from ideas of nation-building and citizenship in 18th-century Europe. Two of the most prominent of today's museums were among the first to open up to the public: the British Museum, in London (1759), and the Louvre, in Paris (1793). Industrialization spread from the United Kingdom to the continent, along with urbanization, the drive for knowledge fueled by the Enlightenment, and the notion of national identity, which fed on colonialism.

Under these conditions, the first global museum boom occurred between roughly the 1780s and the 1900s, led initially by the establishment of national museums in Europe, which used formerly royal collections as manifestations of their power and cultural status (see chapter 3 for a discussion of China's imperial collections). In The Netherlands, the National Art Gallery was founded in The Hague in 1800 and moved to Amsterdam in 1808 to eventually become the Rijksmuseum. The Prado Museum in Madrid, commissioned by Charles III, opened in 1819 to display part of the royal collection. In Berlin, what is now known as the Museumsinsel started as a picture gallery to house the collection of Prussian Frederick William III in 1830. Only six years later, the Alte Pinakothek opened in Munich to display the painting collections of the dukes of Wittelsbach. By 1852, the major collection of the Russian tsars had been made available to the public at the Hermitage Museum in St. Petersburg.

The Enlightenment pursuit of encyclopedic knowledge gave rise to the first comprehensive natural history and science museums. The Victoria and Albert Museum and the Science Museum, both in South Kensington, London, were founded to house the collections exhibited at the Great Exhibition of 1851 (the first World's Fair) with the stated purpose of mass education and raising the skills of the working class to improve the competitiveness of Britain's industrial products.

Imperialism had the effect of expanding the boom both at home and abroad. The treasure that was brought home would stimulate more than curiosity; it could reinforce the perception of the superiority of the colonizers. In the actual colonies, museums were places to better understand the land and people under control. In Jakarta, Indonesia, the Dutch founded the Batavia Society of Arts and Science in 1778, which in time became the Central Museum of Indonesian Culture and finally part of the National Museum of Indonesia. The origins of the Indian Museum in Calcutta were similar: it evolved from the collections of the Asiatic Society of Bengal, which was established in 1784 by Sir William Jones, an Anglo-Welsh philologist, to enhance and further the cause of Oriental research. In America, Brazil's National Museum in Rio de Janeiro (recently destroyed by fire) was opened to the public as the Royal Museum in 1818 at the initiative of King João VI of Portugal; the zoological collection of the Pictou Academy in Nova Scotia, Canada, was founded by Scotsman Thomas McCulloch in 1816 and opened to the public around 1822.

About 100 museums were established in Britain between 1860 and 1887, while 50 museums opened throughout Germany in the 5 years from 1876 to 1880—these institutions possessed a clear educational mandate. In the United States, in 1846 the government received the sum of half a million dollars from the estate of James Smithson to found "for the increase and diffusion of knowledge," the Smithsonian Institution. Another renowned U.S. institution opened shortly after in New York in 1872, the Metropolitan Museum of Art.

During this first stage—prior to the 20th century—comparably fewer museums opened in Africa and Asia, with notable exceptions such as the zoological collection of Sir Andrew Smith in Cape Town, South Africa (1825), the Tokyo National Museum and National Science Museum (1872), the National Museum of Thailand (originally founded as the Grand Palace at Bangkok in 1874), or the Ziccawei Museum (1868) and the Shanghai Museum (1871), founded respectively by French missionaries and British expatriates in Shanghai.

China experienced its own first museum boom a little later and for a short period of time, between the year 1905—with the opening of the first public museum set up by a Chinese person, the Nantong Museum—and the foundation of the People's Republic of China in 1949, by which time emblematic museums such as the Palace Museum (1925) and the Nanjing Museum (1948) were in place, alongside more than 200 other museums (see chapter 3).

The Second Museum Boom: 1980 to Today

There was no museum building boom in the West and East during a period of global catastrophes—a depression and two world wars. Qualitative achievement rather than quantitative growth marked the period 1900 to 1980, leading to the development of a museum profession in place of gifted amateurs. National and international policies were developed, museum advocacy organizations proliferated (such as the American Association of Museums founded in 1906, and the International Council of Museums in 1946), while the roles of museums expanded beyond preservation, documentation, and education to encompass leisure, children's education (especially from the 1930s), and debate.

The second museum boom, which continues to the date of publication of this book, started in the 1980s, ignited by a combination of several factors: urban regeneration, the emergence of new forms of art, and the growth of private collectors and cultural philanthropy.

Human beings became urban people in 2008 when for the first time in history more than half the world's population lived in cities. In the global north and west, this had long been the case with the populations at 80 percent urban. By the early part of the 21st century, cities are accounting for 80 percent of global GDP. For China it is only in the last six years that urban population has exceeded rural. With densification of cities and a shift from industrial economies to knowledge-based ones, urban regeneration takes center stage for a number of reasons such as improving the quality of life for the incoming new residents, who are "knowledge" and service workers (as distinct from industrial workers, who are now pushed to the margins); to compete for talent, technology, and tourism; and to protect real estate values.[5]

These new urban goals require strategies for urban revitalization and city branding, which more often than not have involved building museums. The first cities to successfully put this strategy in motion—Bilbao, Spain, with the Guggenheim Museum in 1997; Salford, England, with the Lowry in 2000—were postindustrial cities with high rates of unemployment, degraded urban ecosystems, and low self-esteem that were able to improve their situations by rebuilding themselves with substantial new and innovative iconic cultural institutions.

The Guggenheim Museum in Bilbao—the crown jewel of a holistic urban transformation that involved a new underground network and the regeneration of the riverbank—created more than 1,000 full-time jobs across the hospitality, creative, and knowledge sectors; underpinned 4,400 existing jobs in the city; and led to an eightfold increase in tourist visits.[6] Such was the success of this strategy that the term "Bilbao effect" was coined, and hundreds of local governments around the world have attempted to replicate its benefits—some with more success than others.

It is not accidental that the notion of museums as destinations has coincided with the boom in global tourism, one of the fastest-growing economic sectors,[7] and the rise of "starchitects" (designing a museum constitutes one of the most prestigious commissions for an architect). Ultimately, local governments have to hope that their museums compete on a global and regional level in the realm of branding, soft power, and talent recruitment. This book demonstrates that China's museum building boom is consistent with these global trends.

Another region of the world that has embraced museum building for the purposes of city branding and cultural status is the Arabian Gulf, where the oil economy provides the fuel for a future they see as in tourism (the Dubai airport surpassed Heathrow in 2014 as the busiest international airport in the world), technology, and real estate. As a result, the cities of this region have been able to build an arts ecosystem from a standing start: by 2008 the region ushered in the age of the extraordinary museums following the opening in Doha, Qatar, of the Museum of Islamic Art (2008) and MATHAF: Arab Museum of Modern Art (2010), both initiatives of the ruling family that dominated the global auction market between 2006 and 2014. Other Gulf nations and regions also embarked on the race with notable examples including the Sharjah Biennial (Sharjah, UAE, 2009); the Etihad Museum (Dubai, UAE, 2017); the recently opened and widely acclaimed Louvre Abu Dhabi (Abu Dhabi, UAE, 2017); and the King Abdulaziz Centre for World Culture, a project of the world's largest energy company—Saudi Aramco—which was inaugurated in 2017 in Saudi Arabia.

As the global south and east urbanize, we can expect rapid development of museums there as well. Meanwhile the museums of the "old world" compete to establish branches and partnerships with these emerging cities and their museums in part to help pay the overheads of their own museum booms.

The second museum boom has been stimulated by the emergence of new forms of art that arise in response to the human need to reflect on, and adjust to, an ever-accelerating pace of change. In a knowledge economy, art and museums become tools for solace, learning, and financial gain—as "content" for sale on the commercial market where fortunes can be made and lost.[8] The private sector[9] is therefore playing an increasing role in this museum boom.

One museum that has taken on the role of displaying new forms of art and providing thought-provoking controversial experiences is MONA—Museum of Old and New Art, in Hobart, Tasmania, an island off the southern tip of Australia. A private initiative, MONA opened in 2011 to display the David Walsh collection and immediately shifted the art world's attention toward the Southern Hemisphere for its unique approach: "We believe things like art history and the individual artist's intention are interesting and important—but only alongside other voices and approaches that remind us that art, after all, is made and consumed by real, complex people—whose motives mostly are obscure, even to themselves. That, and we want you to have fun. Settle in at the Void Bar. Have a drink."[10]

Private philanthropy, often in collaboration with government and local authorities, has also created innovative places for art such as island art complexes, which have become retreats where one can navigate through monumental sculptures, immersive installations, and land art. Examples include Jeju Island in South Korea; the Finnish islet Sarvisalo, which functions as an "art colony"; and the art islands of Japan's Inland Sea.

A major trend of the 1990s was the ascendance of contemporary art, which became the art market's biggest growth sector. "The number of auctions, art fairs and galleries dealing in that genre has grown enormously to accommodate this burgeoning market."[11] Additionally, existing museums dealing with other periods of art history have extended their missions to cover contemporary art as well, leading to a boom of museum expansions and the appearance of satellite venues devoted solely to this new form of art. These facilities also required new standards to properly display the large-scale formats, time-based media, or participatory practices that contemporary art demands.

A majority of existing art museums have gone through an expansion in the last 25 years to accommodate new forms of art, and most of them have sought renowned architects to create groundbreaking iconic structures. A well-known example of a contemporary art museum "satellite" is Tate Modern in London, the latest addition to the Tate network of galleries. The Tate Gallery (now Tate Britain) needed to expand in response to a growing collection, audiences with new needs, and the changing nature of the arts. As a result, a new museum—Tate Modern—was opened in 2000 to become one of the largest and most renowned museums of modern and contemporary art in the world. It is often used as a case study for urban regeneration for the successful conversion of a disused historic power station. The title of the book documenting the building of Tate Modern is *Power into Art*. Now disused power stations have been transformed into art, urban improvement, and real estate in urban settings around the globe, including Toronto, Sydney, Istanbul, and Shanghai.

The last 25 years have seen an exponential increase in the number of private museums. Whereas in the past private collectors preferred to donate collections to existing museums, a significant number today create their own museums. These initiatives often involve contemporary art. Some are fueled by the desire to be involved in public education, others by the art and real estate markets or a combination of all of these. "The Private Art Museum Report"[12] counts 317 privately founded contemporary art museums in the world; over 70 percent were founded after 2000 and nearly a fifth of these private museums have opened within the last five years.

The global north and west have been experiencing the museum boom phenomenon for some 250 years, albeit with peaks and lows. The periods of rapid acceleration of museum development have seen enormous changes in the purposes, processes, and even the architecture of museums. The downtimes have been periods of consolidation and professionalization. China is experiencing most of these changes in one very concentrated period and at a scale never before seen in history.

3

A BRIEF HISTORY OF CHINESE MUSEUMS TO 1949

Duan Yong

A country with a vast territory, large population, and abundant cultural and natural resources, China was able to sustain a substantial gentry class quite early in its history. These aristocrats, scholar-artists, officials, and other landed individuals both appreciated and consumed fine art and decorative objects. Since ancient times, self-cultivation and the appreciation of culture were intertwined with the ethic of the *junzi* or gentleman. The civil service exams, which required mastery of ancient texts in order to grant access to the upper echelons of the court, set up the notion of "appreciation and understanding of culture" as an inherent good, so that today even a child in an impoverished village not only knows the names of a few poets and philosophers, but can even recite a few lines of poetry by heart.

This legacy of connoisseurship began to assume the form of something similar to a museum some 2,500 years ago when, some scholars believe, we have evidence of the very first museum in China. Founded by Duke Ai of the state of Lu in 478 BCE, the museum consisted of a temple in honor of Confucius that featured articles, artifacts, and archives relevant to the ideas and life of Confucius. The Confucius temple can be regarded as the earliest museum for commemorative purposes, a kind of "proto museum,"[1] which like the Musaeum (Temple and the Muses) created by Ptolemy in 284 BCE (along with the great library of Alexandria) offered a prototype for museums in both the East and the West.

The Confucius temple contained the carriage, clothes, and utensils that had once been held in the hands of the sage, and the purpose of these objects was to allow people to pay respect to Confucius, to study how to conduct rituals and perform ceremonies. Art historian Richard Vinograd writes that Confucian academies as educational institutions also often housed collections of stone steles upon which important texts were inscribed.[2] Qufu, the Confucius family temple in Shandong, has a collection that dates to 156 CE, and another Confucian temple in northwest Xi'an collected a veritable "forest" of these steles that forms the collection of the "Forest of Stone Steles" at the Beilin Museum in Xi'an. Today you can visit Qufu or the Beilin Museum and see visitors relaxing in the shaded courtyards gazing up in awe at these ancient tablets thanks to the work of these early proto-museum curators.

Vinograd also writes that Buddhist and Taoist temples served an important role in both preserving and educating the public. Housed in historically significant architecture, these temples featured permanent collections of both painting and statuary that select visitors could enjoy. Like contemporary art museums today, these temples actually helped define the artistic canon of the Tang and Song dynasties, not only by displaying work but also by commissioning art from the most sought-after artists at the time. Artists such as Wu Daozi, the Tang dynasty painter, attracted throngs of onlookers keen to see the artist creating masterpieces on-site. In addition to temples, other public venues such as teahouses and painting shops frequently displayed works of important art historical value that visitors were able to view.[3]

Despite this tradition of proto-museums, there was a relative lack of awareness on the subject of how to transform privately owned collections into public ones. Scholar Marzia Varutti writes that the proto-museums developed differently from Western museums in that they often didn't contain specimen collections, but they did include artifacts relating to certain figures or popular deities such as Mazu—the guardian of the seas.[4] That is why the fledgling museums of ancient times didn't evolve into modern public museums but more as shrines to enable public remembrance. Given the emphasis placed on ritual in ancient times, this is not surprising.

It isn't until the mid-19th century that we see the museums that are recognizable to us today, emerging in various treaty ports, opened by foreigners, primarily for a foreign audience. Notable among these was the Xujiahui Natural Sciences Museum (Ziccawei Museum), opened in 1868 by French Jesuit missionary Pierre Heude. Like many facilities run by the Jesuits in Shanghai (for instance, the Tushanwan Art School), the museum was not public but more of a research base for Heude, who was a trained zoologist, keen on collecting and studying specimens from all over Asia.[5] In 1871, the Royal Asiatic Society (RAS), a British society of Asian studies scholars and enthusiasts, founded the "Shanghai Museum"[6] housed in an art deco building near Shanghai's Bund (now the Rockbund Museum). This was funded by local philanthropists and the Shanghai Municipal Council (the colonial government of the Shanghai International Settlement). The RAS was more interested in serving resident expatriates than the Chinese community, and most of its interpretation was provided in English. At one point, the museum's fund-raising needs provoked the inclusion of Chinese labels to reach out to elite local donors, but it still had little Chinese support given its paltry collection of antiquities.[7]

Nonetheless, many visitors responded enthusiastically to these new types of museums established by Western organizations. They were, in a sense, seen as "foreign wonders" and "disseminators of modernity." The Chinese word for museum *bowuguan* 博物馆 meaning "a hall brimming with plentiful objects" encapsulated the *wunderkammer* concept[8] and was coined by Li Gui, a customs officer who had visited the 1876 Expo in Philadelphia. The museum, with its inherent "imported status," writes Varutti, possesses a kind of tension associated with the question of how to "domesticate this exotic transplant," one imbued with negative colonial associations.[9]

Figure 4 The Nantong Museum (1905), China's first modern museum founded by a Chinese national, Zhang Jian. *Photography: Chao Zhen. Photos courtesy: China Museums Associations Architecture and Technology Committee, "China Museum Architecture Archive," and the Nanjing Museum*

In 1876, the Qing government established the first natural science museum at the Tongwenguan (or School of Combined Learning). The Tongwenguan Science Museum was the first publicly-owned science museum in China based in a college, as the Tongwenguan was a school dedicated to the study of foreign languages and knowledge.

Almost thirty years later, we have what is widely considered to be the first modern comprehensive Chinese museum, the Nantong Museum—a private museum founded in 1905 by intellectual and industrialist Zhang Jian. Zhang was inspired by the model of the Japanese Imperial Palace Museum and by the Universal Fair in Japan. He had originally wanted to establish a Palace Museum in Beijing but was denied by the Qing court, who would ironically, only a decade later, lose most of their possessions to the state.

Zhang instead set his sights on something more modest but by no means unimpressive. The museum was not only the first modern museum in China but also the first *private* museum, as it was solely funded by Zhang's family. At 666 square meters, it might be considered small by today's standards but nonetheless contained several buildings, a botanical garden, and a zoo along with artistic, biological, and historical collections. Today's museum professionals would be heartened to learn that the Nantong Museum *also* struggled with the challenges of protecting its collection, with unruly visitors touching, breaking, and absconding with artifacts and specimens.

Beyond its pedagogical functions, the Nantong Museum played a pivotal role in helping strengthen both morale and Chinese identity at the time when the country was facing serious threats from Japan.[10] The function of museums, since the founding of the Republic of China in 1912, has largely been related to patriotic endeavors: projecting a cohesive national image and nurturing a national consciousness. At this time, a wave of state-owned museums were constructed; among them are earlier iterations of some key museums today, including the Palace Museum.

A total of 231 museums (both state-owned and privately owned) had been established in China by 1936, which was quite an impressive number for the time. These museums were public in a way that the previous proto-museums were not. Vinograd writes that prior to this period, the private collections, imperial collections, and the temples fulfilled the function of the museum but to a much narrower public, which consisted largely of aristocrats, officials, and literary or artistic personalities.[11]

Figure 5 The Shanghai Municipal History Museum (2018) opened in the former location of the Shanghai Art Museum. *Photography: Rebecca Catching*

Unlike the temples, certain types of modern museums did not only focus on displaying beautiful objects but rather attempted to explain the world in a systematic manner. For instance, the Nantong Museum very much replicated the structures of knowledge seen in the foreign settlement museums, dividing the collection into archaeology, history, and natural sciences. In taking this scientific rationalist approach, the museum wanted to focus more on China's modernity and scientific progress than its glorious past.[12]

The Republican Era brought with it a new thirst for modern ideas but also a new "availability of collections" that helped fuel momentum for what was China's first museum boom. The development of three influential museums in the Forbidden City, the Gallery of Antiquities, the Palace Museum, and the Natural History Museum, was marked by the impassioned power struggles between warlords, the throne, and the emerging Republican government.

The first of these museums within the palace, actually proto-national museums, was the *Guwu Chenliesuo* 古物陈列所 or Gallery of Antiquities, also commonly known in English as the Government Museum. It was opened in the southern court of the Forbidden City in 1914. Its collection featured artifacts from the Chengde and Shenyang Palaces. Symbolically, its physical location—between the imperial family's quarters and the proposed residence of warlord Yuan Shikai (also a self-proclaimed president of the Republic)—reflected the shared balance of power at the time. Both sides had a keen interest in these cultural objects and the legitimacy they could bestow.[13] The Republican government also had a very practical objective in mind, which was to claim real estate in the Forbidden City to prevent the royals from being reinstated to the throne.[14]

Beyond these ulterior motives, there were some genuine advocates for museums, including Zhang Jian (Nantong Museum) and Jin Liang, the director of the Imperial Lodge in Shenyang who pleaded unsuccessfully with child emperor Puyi to establish a museum to house the imperial possessions. Caught in the maelstrom of the conflicting forces, monarchy, Republicans, and warlords, the founders of the Palace Museum and the Gallery of Antiquities sought to establish the museums covertly so as not to ruffle imperial feathers. But during this process, the abdication of the throne put these vast collections in jeopardy.

The imperial collections were spread across a vast territory in various palaces and hunting lodges. When 233 items were seized from antique markets in Beijing and Shanghai—which had "slipped through the hands" of Xiong Xilai, the military governor of Hebei—the urgency of creating some viable system of protection was made clear. On top of this, China's cultural heritage was at risk due to the numerous foreign museum expeditions roving throughout the country and procuring objects for their own collections, objects that were all-too-easily obtainable. The Republican government moved swiftly to transfer the 119,500 objects from various imperial residences to Beijing with the plans of future storage and exhibition. These objects included jades, bronzes, clocks, and even a large number of live deer.[15]

These artifacts, minus the deer, of course, were exhibited in the Hall of Military Prowess, Wuyingdian, piled on top of each other pell-mell in a fashion that author Lu Xun has likened to an antiques store. Tickets for the Gallery of Antiquities were relatively expensive, roughly a third of a month's salary for the average Beijing resident, yet students were allowed free admittance—a very forward-thinking policy for the time.

Once the royals were installed at the Summer Palace, the Palace Museum could take possession of the inner courtyard, representing a symbolic move whereby imperial space was eclipsed by public space. When the Palace Museum opened on October 10, 1925, 50,000 visitors flocked to the palace over a period of two days, no doubt keen to see how the imperial household lived. This "proto-blockbuster" reflected a growing trend toward "accessibility," which was enshrined in the very name of the museum, *Gugong Gongli Bowuguan*," whereby the word *gongli* or "public" is inserted into the title of Palace Museum. This was a political move on the part of the Republican government, and debates were had to lower the admission fees, to make the museum even *more* accessible. This move put pressure on the Gallery of Antiquities, which aimed to cater to a wealthier demographic—the competition provoking the museum to provide a more sophisticated visitor experience with better layout and labels, which in turn drove the museum to invite scholars into the collection to properly study the artifacts.

The third museum in the Forbidden City was the Natural History Museum, which took over the Duan Gate. Unlike its two counterparts, it was not blessed with opulent collections and thus distinguished itself by its ambitious attitude toward collecting, focusing on archaeology. In 1921, it sent out a team of excavators to a Song dynasty ruin in Henan to bring back 200 objects—largely seen as the first museum-led excavation.[16] The museum was ambitious in other ways as well, touring one of their exhibitions to Germany in 1913 and offering free admission to the public in 1926. It is now part of the National Museum of China.

Though the imperial possessions were now protected within the walls of the Forbidden City, the shifting sands of the Republican Era would keep the custodians of China's heritage on their toes. The invasion of Manchuria by the Japanese caused anxiety about the collections in Beijing, and moves were made to have the collection moved south and west. Over 100,000 objects were packed up to be sent to Nanjing, Chongqing, Shanghai, and many other places. Trunks were carted out of the palace in the middle of the night so as not to alarm the Beijing public. This virtual caravan of antiquities moved from city to city like an underground railroad for the clandestine transport of fine treasures. After the Japanese surrender, the treasures made their way back to the Central Museum in Nanjing, where the KMT departed with part of the collection—852 crates that now form the collection of the Palace Museum in Taipei.[17]

These three museums loom large in the narrative of Chinese museology as providing foundational models for the museums we see today. What is perhaps most impressive is not the objects but these early curators and directors, and the heavy responsibility they bore. They had not only to master the skills of exhibition making, research, cataloging, archaeological work, and international exchange but also had to negotiate with a changing society that, until that point, had not had experience with these kinds of public institutions. On top of this, they had the challenging task of preserving their collections from theft by the Japanese, the Western museums, and sometimes their own countrymen. This takes the roles of "curator" as "custodian" to a completely different level. Many of the curators of the Palace Museum distinguished themselves in staying behind in the Forbidden City to negotiate with the Japanese not to destroy what was left, while others pleaded with the Kuomintang to prevent the objects from being sent to Taiwan. This first generation of Chinese museum workers was clearly a passionate lot, moved by a deep understanding of the aesthetic, political, spiritual, and cultural value of their collections. This spirit is something that lives on in museums today, and also in the hearts and minds of the viewers.

4

A BRIEF HISTORY OF CHINESE MUSEUMS 1949–1995

Song Xiangguang

In 1949, when the People's Republic of China (PRC) was founded, its leaders recognized the importance of preserving the country's history and the role that museums would play in nation-building and scientific and patriotic education. For celebration of the anniversary of the PRC, the Museum of the Chinese Revolution and Museum of Chinese History located across from the Great Hall of the People in Tiananmen Square and completed in 1959 would serve as a model for other museums at the time. Chinese museums in that era saw history through the prism of "class struggle" and historical materialism. But the Reform and Opening-Up in 1978 saw a change in the core function of the museum, which was now tasked with developing the Socialist economy and mobilizing all sectors of society to rally to the cause of modernization.

From an early time, the state played an important role as a steward of the museums, holding frequent conferences to draw up ideological guidelines and also help standardize the sector. In 1977, the State Cultural Relics Bureau (its current name: National Cultural Heritage Administration, NCHA) held conferences in Harbin, Daqing, and Suzhou to discuss the role of museums after the Cultural Revolution (1966–1976). During these meetings, they drew up a set of guidelines to strengthen the management and preservation of museum collections and improve professional team building.[1]

In the early 1980s, China began to develop a growing diversity of museums that focused on specific themes rather than trying to tell one overarching story. Small and medium-size theme museums sprang up, which greatly enlivened the landscape. Cultural artifacts departments set up museums in vacant historic sites. Some administrative departments of the government that focus on specific areas of industry established industrial museums, covering topics such as silk, post and telecommunications, sports, stamps, and coins. In September 1988, the first science museum opened its doors; the China Science and Technology Museum was opened in Beijing, focusing on Chinese achievements in science, including such innovations as the compass, gunpowder, and bronze smelting and casting technology. Its second hall, which would open 12 years later, would take a broader look at science—including topics such as energy, information technology, and life sciences.

The 1980s and 1990s brought a loosening of government control, and museums were given more flexibility on operations and financial management; this freedom, it was hoped, would provide the necessary vitality to improve the level of management at museums. During the Reform, a management system based on post and position was established with an incentive system linked to individual contributions of museum employees. Some museums and Opening Up carried out profitable activities, the benefits of which were returned to the museums and the staff. These measures helped mobilize the staff, improving their level of enthusiasm. This entrepreneurial spirit, at the time when the market economy was just beginning to bloom again, caused quite a stir in museum circles. There were extensive discussions throughout the field, and the authorities decided that the museum's social function should not be impacted by its financial activities.

The professionalization of the field was greatly aided by the founding of the Chinese Museum Society in 1983, a precursor of today's Chinese Museums Association (CMA). The society edited and published professional publications such as the *China Museum* (quarterly) and *China Museum Newsletter* to introduce international museum trends and collect and analyze the experiences of domestic museums. This was particularly important because due to language barriers, cost, and restricted access to foreign materials, Chinese museum professionals in the 1980s had little access to international information. This access to international museum practice was greatly aided in 1983 with China's joining the International Council of Museums, sending 13 members of the society to participate in an ICOM conference in London.

With this growing internationalism, the influence of the Cultural Revolution faded from the halls of the museum, replaced by an emphasis on cultural undertakings—with the aim of building advanced international-caliber museums with Chinese characteristics. These "characteristics" included more architectural specificity, with newly built museums reflecting the local architectural vernacular or regional history and culture. For example, the Shaanxi History Museum kicked off this trend of individualized architectural typologies, with its Tang dynasty style form. Other new buildings such as the Shanghai Museum made waves with its unique round architecture shaped like a "ding" or bronze cooking vessel, as did the Henan Museum for its distinct pyramidal form.

In the 1990s exhibitions began to focus on particular elements of regional culture, regional civilization, and major historical events. These museums not only explored more specific themes than their predecessors, but also wove these themes throughout the structure of the exhibition. Notable exhibitions included "Five Thousand Years of Civilization in the Middle and Lower Reaches of Yangtze River" (Nanjing Museum, 1989); "Seven Thousand Years of Zhejiang" (Zhejiang Provincial Museum, 1993); and "The Light of Ancient Culture in Henan" (Henan Museum, 1998). This is unique in that exhibition design in China often aims

Figure 6 The Shaanxi History Museum (1991, Xi'an) was one of the first major large-scale (65,000 square meters) state museums. The building is Tang dynasty in style, as Xi'an was the capital of the Tang dynasty, world famous for its proximity to the archaeological site where the Terra Cotta Warriors are displayed. *Photography: Chao Zhen. Photo courtesy: China Museums Association, Architecture and Technology Committee, China Archive of Museum Architecture, and the Nanjing Museum*

Song Xiangguang

Figure 7 The Nanjing Museum (1933, 1999, 2000), established by the educator Cai Yuanpei. The Nanjing Museum's development was interrupted by the Japanese invasion and the following civil war. During the chaos, it lost half of its collection to the Kuomintang. *Photography: Chao Zhen. Photo courtesy: Chinese Museums Association Architecture and Technology Committee, China Archive of Museum Architecture, and the Nanjing Museum*

for an aesthetic that tends toward a dehistoricization in the presentation of antiquities. Rather than focusing on the specific details of the time, the emphasis is on the presentation of China as an ancient nation, "continuous, glorious and worthy of pride," a "timeless cultural entity" as described by scholar Marzia Varutti.

As is the case in the West, the collection of art objects has always been a means for individuals to display their status and culture. Although many collections of art and objects were lost in the sands of history, the 1980s began to see the revival of private collections. In November 1992, the Shanghai Sihai Teapot Museum was one of the first museums to gain official approval under the Shanghai Culture Management Commission. In December 1996, the Beijing Municipal Administration of Cultural Heritage approved the establishment of three more non-state-owned museums, namely the Museum of Ancient Pottery and Civilization, the He Yang and Wu Xi Modern Painting Museum, and the Guanfu Classical Art Museum, which

has now become an impressive example of the capabilities of private museums.

While many museums focus on history and antiquities and Han culture, in the 1990s attempts were made to introduce narratives that addressed China's ethnic minorities. China has 55 officially recognized minorities, the most numerous being the Zhuang, Hui, Manchu, Uighur, and Miao. The distinct regional cultures of these minority groups is often leveraged to create tourism opportunities and drive regional development in provinces such as Yunnan, Xinjiang, Tibet, Sichuan, Guizhou, Ningxia, and Inner Mongolia. These regions have distinct cultures based on their geography. The people who inhabit these regions have unique customs, languages, dress, cuisine, and faiths. The boom in ecomuseums offers opportunities for new models. Based on the concepts popularized in the 1970s by Georges Henri Rivière and Hugues de Varine, these museums espoused a more natural and holistic approach to cultural heritage.

This was a relatively new model in China at the time and was tested out in a number of communities in Guizhou Province in Southwest China, where 37 percent of the population is ethnic minorities, including Buyi, Miao, and Dong. This regional museum boom, beyond bringing tourists, also served the benefit of providing better cultural facilities to these underserved populations. These ecomuseums built in 1995 include the Suoga Ecomuseum (Longhorn Miao people); the Buyi Museum of Zhenshan (Buyi people); Dong Ecomuseum of Tang'an (Dong people); and Ancient City Ecomuseum in Longli. They were founded after in-depth investigations by museum scholars from China and Norway and served to help the progress of museological practice around the country.[2]

The Guizhou ecomuseums serve an important function in introducing new models, going beyond the old template of the minority museum that is merely a collection of ethnic costumes hanging limply in display cases. China has always had a slightly tense relationship with the other groups that occupy its great land mass. But as Chinese audiences become hungry for new content, objects, and stories, they may look increasingly to understand the incredible diversity that exists within this historically rich and dynamic country.

Song Xiangguang

5

THE MUSEALIZATION OF CHINA

Sofia Bollo and Yu Zhang

Museums in contemporary China are undergoing a reconfiguration of policies in order to adapt to the needs of the market economy, for which new legislation is attempting to pave the way. In the programs that Chinese museums develop, the need to comply with the different missions of museums (as defined by International Council of Museums [ICOM]) is doubled with Chinese political directives. Meanwhile, new joint projects in the museum and heritage sectors, constant technological advancements, international exhibitions, and cultural exchanges are increasing—less as a need for economic sustainability than as a means to establish Chinese cultural diplomacy. If "musealization" is understood as the operation of "trying to extract, physically or conceptually, something from its natural or cultural environment, transforming it into a '*musealium*' or 'museum object,'" it can be argued that China is currently undergoing a "musealization" process.[1]

The Recent Boom: Motivating Factors

The opening of new museums can be explained by a number of factors. First, the development of museums in China is the result of favorable measures in terms of financial and cultural policy. The increase in the budget allocated to culture was pivotal for the growth of museums. Some 140 billion RMB in public funds was allocated to cultural heritage protection from 2011 to 2015. In addition to central government support, public museums received subsidies from local government, while private museums could apply for local government funding on a project basis.

These economic incentives were accompanied by other initiatives: (1) local councils started looking to the Bilbao model to attract tourists with new cultural landmarks through the extension of existing museums; (2) the opening of trade or industrial museums by (former) state-owned companies; and (3) the introduction of specialized museums, e.g., science and technology, natural history, art, contemporary art, folk art, ethnology, industrial heritage, 21st-century heritage, intangible heritage, as well as the multiplication of private museums. Museum development is also due to an increase in archaeological excavations: new archaeological discoveries often lead to the establishment of site museums. By 2006, the NCHA listed a total of 2,351 archaeological sites and historical monuments as National Major Heritage Protection Units.

Re-envisioning Heritage Sites

The value of heritage has also been applied to local economic development through the promotion of cultural tourism. Tourism is developing as a leisure activity within an expanding economic industry, as will be discussed later in the chapter.

A notable example of musealization and cultural tourism can be found in the "2016 No. 1 Central Document"—an annual report on developments in key policy published by the Central Committee of the Communist Party of China and the State Council.[2] In this report, the government emphasizes the importance of preserving historic settlements and building "beautiful and liveable villages," which has led to the revitalization of Chinese traditional villages. Prominent Chinese architects have been involved in these projects to advise on the consolidation of old houses, replanning of the villages, and creation or repurposing of spaces, especially for community and cultural activities.

Figure 8 Artisans Zhang Xiaoqi and Zhang Xiaomeng holding bottles of "Xihe Liangyou" (high-quality camellia oil) at Xihe Cereals and Oils Museum and Village Activity Center (2014). The project puts the local architectural community at the center of the museum experience. *Photo Courtesy 3andwich Design*

This requires the villagers' needs to be taken into account throughout the whole process. Such projects were launched even before the government directives were made official. For example, in Henan Province, a Cereals and Oils Museum and Village Activity Center was created. Some villages are opting for cultural tourism with the hope to attract visitors, whether domestic or foreign, which in return will help create jobs and generate income.

The Wuzhen model is one example of a revitalized village. With its international arts festival, attended by renowned contemporary artists, Wuzhen, a town of around 60,000 people in the eastern province of Zhejiang, has become a talking point. Following years of infrastructural renovation that began in 1999, Wuzhen even hosts a number of high-profile events, including a contemporary art festival, a theater festival, and the World Internet Conference.[3] Wuzhen has evolved from a water town into a popular tourist destination—half preservation, half recreation. No doubt its tasteful execution has made it a model for other water towns to emulate.

Figure 9 The Xihe Cereals and Oils Museum and Village Activity Center (2014), Xinyang in Henan Province. Designed by 3andwich Design/He Wei Studio, the museum was commissioned by the rural cooperative. *Photo Courtesy 3andwich Design*

Sofia Bollo and Yu Zhang

New Trends

Within the Thirteenth Five-Year Plan (2015–2020), "cultural industries"—a term first introduced in a central policy document in 2010's Eleventh Five-Year Plan—are expected to become a pillar in the national economy in the coming five years. Museums in contemporary China have recently been undergoing a policy reconfiguration to adapt to the needs of the dynamic market economy, alongside reconceptualization of cultural heritage values.[4]

The revised Cultural Relics Law came into effect in 2015.[5] The amendments set the foundations for the professional management of museums, encouraging them to diversify their income resources by collaborating with private entities and by setting up boards of trustees. Another novel and crucial reform allows for the creation of a museum without authorization. Nevertheless, newly opened museums need to be registered after their establishment, especially if the term "museum" is intended to be used in their name. NCHA is adding more regulations with regard to the creation of non-state-owned museums and requires local heritage institutions to coordinate the creation of new museums.[6]

The Thirteenth Five-Year Plan

As part of the Key Tasks for National Cultural Heritage Administration in 2017, under the country's Thirteenth Five-Year Plan, an annual evaluation system will take into account the protection of cultural heritage at local levels, and local authorities will be held accountable for negligence if they fail to protect cultural heritage.

In the Five-Year Plan, other measures introduced are:

- encouraging the creation of cultural merchandise (so far, income from museum shops and products represents 10 percent of the global income of museums);

- increasing employment and the number of qualified museum workers in the cultural heritage sector;

- increasing protection of immovable cultural heritage and establishing a compensation scheme for cities abundant in such cultural resources and for private collectors who want to conserve their valuable objects;

- stressing preventive conservation; and

- encouraging more social involvement in the cultural sector economy.

Cultural Merchandise

To support organizations in developing cultural merchandise, the State Council has issued general guidelines for several departments, including the Ministry of Culture and Tourism and the Ministry of Finance. These documents encourage national and regional cultural organizations (including museums, art museums, and libraries) to experiment with cultural merchandise and allow them to set the retail prices, to license intellectual property, and to establish commercial enterprises. On a national level, the other general directives that are to be applied to museums are "Internet + Chinese Civilisation" or "Let Cultural Relics Tell Their Stories."[7] Museum games, mobile applications, merchandising products inspired by museum collections, as well as edutainment are among many examples of how museums implement the policy of "Internet + Chinese Civilisation" or "Let Cultural Relics Tell Their Stories."

Cultural Diplomacy and One Belt, One Road

The Thirteenth Five-Year Plan also includes measures to enhance the protection of cultural heritage and its promotion overseas in all channels and at all levels. Several high-level government meetings were held since the outlining of the plan, while top Chinese officials including President Xi Jinping and Prime Minister Li Keqiang also stressed the importance of cultural heritage protection and international cooperation.[8] In July 2016, the Chinese Museums Association, a government-organized NGO supervised by NCHA, created an online platform to facilitate the exchange of information among museum networks.[9] As it is advertised on the website, the initiative is "a bridge between Chinese museums and their international partners for exhibition exchanges."[10] The platform introduces Chinese exhibitions to the world and showcases international exhibitions for Chinese museums, nurturing international dialogue by encouraging more Chinese artifacts to be shown in foreign institutions via a "China in Cultural Relics" program.

A clear example of how culture and heritage play a role in international cooperation is also illustrated through policies emerging from the Silk Road, a "cultural route" that enabled cultural exchanges and produced a shared heritage. Its most recent reworking in international diplomacy is called "One Belt, One Road (OBOR)."[11] Launched in 2013, this geopolitical initiative is also intertwined with cultural diplomacy.[12] Nurturing a sense of shared history in specific regions creates political and economic cooperation and mutual loyalty. Scholars believe that "heritage diplomacy" will increasingly allow for the reshaping of history, trade, infrastructures, and even security across countries.

New museums, cultural heritage protection projects, exhibitions, festivals, and intangible heritage initiatives can all apply for the Silk Road Fund, a state-owned investment fund founded in 2014. Notable examples include a joint excavation mission between Chinese and

Uzbekistani archaeologists since 2012. This is China's largest archaeological project in a foreign country. The mission is coordinated by the relevant Academy of Social Sciences in each country, and a museum is planned near the archaeological site.

These new trends, domestic directives, international joint exhibition projects, and cultural exchanges for the museum and heritage sectors, together with constant technological advancements and financial strategic incentives, are implemented to a greater extent, responding to a need to establish cultural rather than economic diplomacy for China.

Governance Segmentation

There are limitations to the current Chinese public museum system reflected in the emerging trends described above. Public museums and tangible cultural heritage are under the supervision of a hierarchical and centralized state administration. There is a geographical hierarchy of Major Heritage Protection Units, divided into three levels within NCHA: National, Provincial, and Municipal/County Major Heritage Protection Units.

Overlapping responsibilities, segmented management across various government and local agencies, or gaps, where no agencies are responsible, represent a major challenge for Chinese museums. For example, art museums, which fall into different categories depending on their collection, are managed differently according to their location; furthermore, there are specific museums administered directly or indirectly by the Chinese Central Military Commission, such as the Chinese Aviation Museum and the Military Museum of the Chinese People's Revolution. University museums present a notable dilemma: they depend on specific universities—which are placed under the Ministry of Education in most cases—that are in general not familiar with museum matters and do not assign them with a dedicated permanent staff. They seldom benefit from support offered to "cultural heritage museums" and do not enjoy fiscal benefits such as tax reduction for the acquisition of museum collections.

External Partnerships

Other actors involved in the museum system include NGOs and GONGOs[13]: the powerful Chinese Association for Science and Technology, with its hundreds of societies, directly or indirectly manages the science and technology museums, botanical gardens, observatories, etc. Meanwhile, some of the most important museums in China answer directly to specific ministries: for example, the Palace Museum, the National Museum, and the National Art Museum report directly to the Ministry of Culture, and

the Geological Museum of China to the Ministry of Land and Resources.

By contrast, most of the state-owned provincial museums are managed locally or regionally, where Chinese provinces tend to compete for financial resources and cultural recognition. This apparent separatism of singular provincial cultural institutes, particularly in archaeological institutions, can be as well considered as a means to gain support and legitimacy from the central government, in what has been called a "regionalist paradigm."[14]

Museums and Cultural Identity

Museums are authorized to interpret national history, make a selection, and create a representation of society for society.[15] In China, traditional concepts of history and civilization are moving toward different functional and educational goals; these exploit the past and multiculturalism as tools for establishing new nationalistic features of Chinese cultural identity that is then promoted and enshrined in comprehensive Chinese public museums.[16]

Present-day Chinese nationalism includes the glorification of cultural remnants of the past in a form of new antiquarianism, which becomes instrumental in nurturing patriotism and promotes the enjoyment of cultural consumerism and leisure activities.[17] Today museums in China remain an important part of the active expression of values and the dissemination of state ideology.

Museums in China are indeed effective education tools. A small survey conducted in 2015 on a selection of public museums in China has shown that visitors generally have a positive attitude toward the exhibition content and messages. Nevertheless, many complaints were registered about museums being too crowded and negatively affecting the overall museum experience.[18] This is another big challenge brought forward by the free-admission policy. In order to overcome the downside of the free-admission policy, many museums in China have therefore decided to set an upper limit for daily visitors. For instance, the Palace Museum has limited its daily visitor number to 80,000 and was the first to decide on a specific closing day each week, to undertake restoration and reparation work.

Investment and Commodification of Cultural Heritage

Compared to the Cultural Relics Law, the China Principles (Principles for the Conservation of Heritage Sites in China, a conservation charter initiated by NCHA, the Getty Conservation Institute, and the Australian Heritage Commission, issued by ICOMOS China and approved by NCHA in 2010) put a stronger emphasis on the economic value of cultural heritage. This assertion encouraged the growth of more public-private partnerships (henceforth, PPPs) in areas of cultural heritage management. A case study of Shandong Province shows how the state is still seeking to divest itself of economic complexities by turning management over to the private sector.[19] PPPs in China usually imply outsourcing, concession, and divestiture. On the managerial level, however, problems connected with the interaction of public and private enterprise are becoming more frequent, as usually, each pursues separate goals.[20] The first 11 PPP pilots in the cultural sector include the construction and management of county-level cultural centers and the development of cultural tourism by constructing heritage parks and new museums. Museums are confronted with the commercialization of public history, which might easily lead to the commodification of cultural heritage.[21]

In many parts of China, historical preservation and real estate investment have resulted in tourism gentrification. Tourism is becoming the main driving force in economic, social, cultural, and lifestyle transformations. One of the best-known private tourism corporations is Shenzhen OCT Tourism Development Co. Their slogan is "Originating in real life and rising above it, discarding the dross and select-ing the essential."[22] In becoming national monuments, it is increasingly likely that archaeological sites will be transformed into large parks and lucrative tourist attractions.[23] Such commercialization and commodification of heritage has led some scholars to describe the country's "museum boom" as an exaggerated form of "musealization," even using the pejorative term "museumification."[24]

Besides this defect, museums in China must contend with other issues such as managerial complexities, national-istic narratives all the while trying to keep up with the increasingly sophisticated tastes of viewers in terms of design, technology, and overall experience. We can expect museums to take full advantage of the various elements of government support offered through Internet+ and OBOR, to develop new cultural products, to use technology to create different kinds of digital experiences, and to further expand their presence abroad through the exchange of artifacts and personnel.

This article was adapted from a longer version originally published in *Museum International*, volume 69, titled "Policy and Impact of Public Museums in China: Exploring New Trends and Challenges."

6

BALANCING RELIC PRESERVATION POLICIES AND THE SOCIAL ROLE OF MUSEUMS

Han Yong

China's first state museums emerged from the ashes of the Qing dynasty and the abdication of the throne by emperor Puyi in 1912. The founding of the first museums was an attempt to awaken the national consciousness of the public, still reeling from the loss of their last emperor. The Palace Museum, erected in 1925, ensured that the symbols of the emperor's power would remain intact, especially because the Forbidden City was one day an imperial residence and the next day a museum. This change from the exclusionary palace to a museum for citizens of a new republic possessed a symbolic significance on par with the opening of the Louvre after the French Revolution.

The objects of the imperial household have an inherent connection to the Chinese people because they are the property of the emperor, who is, according to legend, a descendant of heaven. The severing of the imperial line did not, therefore, sever the connection to these storied objects with the Chinese people. This explains why the Chinese museum sector has revolved around objects and artifacts, which are usually referred to as "relics." Given the degree to which the vicissitudes of history since 1912 have posed many threats to Chinese relics (see chapters 3 and 4), an inseparable bond has developed between relic conservation and the Chinese museum sector.

Indeed there is a dichotomy in both the legal and financial structures of the museum system between the need to support both, and relic conservation was given priority. The Cultural Relics Law, established in 1982, is "rescue focused," with protection a key priority followed by management and appropriate utilization of cultural resources. It took almost 33 years after the establishment of the

Cultural Relics Law for the first Regulations on Museums to, for the first time, define the social role of museums. It states that "museums" refer to nonprofit organizations that collect, protect, and display objects . . . for the purpose of education, research, and appreciation. The purpose of the Cultural Relics Law is to protect objects, while the Regulations on Museums is to cultivate people. This dichotomy has until recently held back museum development.

In the early days of the Reform and Opening-Up, the impulse to conserve met with the conflicting forces of economic development. So many regions were so poor that heritage protection seemed like a luxury. This debate still rages on in museum circles, where we see unprecedented rates of preservation; all the while heritage sites and objects continue to disappear through the illegal destruction of relics. In fact, if we look at this issue from another perspective, we soon discover that cultural heritage can only be preserved if it is used—hiding it away leads to deterioration through neglect and even destruction through theft.

This focus on relics, though noble, has resulted in unintended consequences. For instance, there are significant funds invested in the conservation and repair of relics that exist above ground. But there are many relics that remain in storage, trapped in a vicious cycle whereby they are repaired, then put into storage, then they deteriorate, only to be repaired again years later—without any attempt to interpret them.

Archaeological excavations are often characterized by a practice of ignoring basic cultural relationships and information. Often information about excavations is released with no regard to archaeological protocol, which has led to crises of public opinion due to misreporting and media sensationalism. The antiquities market is now booming, and these public leaks have become a dangerous trend. The rarer an object, the more precious it becomes. Hunting for underappreciated relics has become a trend, and the common understanding is that these objects are precious because of their economic value. Museums are also deeply affected by this environment. Many exhibitions lack rigorous research and interpretation; the relics exhibited are often a motley collection, with no supporting educational and promotional activities or publications. Many exhibitions titled "A Selection from the Exquisite Collection of ____" rarely offer anything exquisite to viewers, and even the tombstone labels of national museums contain a lot of misleading content. Such a situation represents a deviation from desired professional standards. The work of relic preservation and the museum industry have long been plagued by the limitations of the industry and also hangovers from previous eras. For instance,

within the realm of object categorization there exists the designation "miscellaneous"—a designation that is clearly a leftover from the antiques industry of days gone by. Meanwhile, as we see the artistic, scientific, modern, and educational facets of the museum continue to be eroded by different degrees, we see the hyperbolic use of the term "national treasure" applied to various museum collections. This has given birth to a "national treasure mafia"—people working within the system to package and promote fake cultural relics using media reports to frame them as the real thing. The public's understanding of antiquities is often viewed through the lens of prices and value, but museum professionals must be clear about their own responsibilities. To museums, the question of price or economic value is irrelevant. The issues of authenticity and meaning are central.

In the museum sector, there are also museums of science and technology, museums of industry, and nature museums. For these museums, relic classification proves to be

Figure 10 Visitors marvel at the coin collection of the Shanghai Museum (1952, 1996) . *Photography: Rebecca Catching*

Han Yong

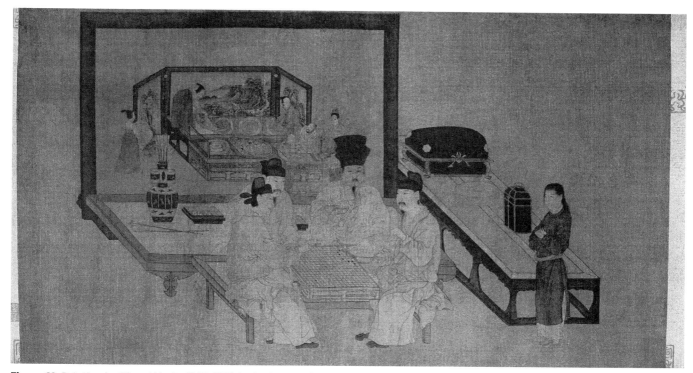

Figure 11 Painting by Zhou Wenju (917–975) in the National Museum of China (2003, 2011, Beijing) depicts nobles playing the game of "go." The preservation of ancient art and artifacts is a challenge facing Chinese museums. *Photo courtesy: Eric Conner*

particularly inconvenient as it falls outside of the realm of expertise. Especially when it comes to responsibility, the classification of relics requires significant reforms. Each object deserves professional treatment, but many collections have suffered losses due to price-related grading systems. This ranking method is outdated and somewhat lazy. Selective conservation should only be an expedient measure used by developing societies.

China's current financial system creates a separation between central and local governments. The main funds of the NCHA come from the central finance department. Although nation-level cultural relics protection units are managed at the local level, the central finance department can directly support their work through earmarking special funds. The problem is that these funds do not cover the costs of personnel or per diems. In addition, few museums can meet the standards required for financial support from the central government. Because China's museum sector is based on municipal, provincial, and national levels, the central finance department is unable to fully support the provincial, municipal, and national-level museums to the level required to meet the needs of access and education. Some provincial museums cannot even guarantee year-round regular opening hours.

Generally speaking, in the past 40 years, both the museum and cultural heritage sectors have achieved remarkable results. However, on a conceptual level, the Chinese museum industry remains fixated on "objects." Many policies, systems, theories, and concepts have to be gradually improved and updated.

For a long time, the Chinese government has designated some museums as "public institutions." These fortunate institutions enjoy full funding from the central finance department, while some balance state funding with earned revenue. In recent years, the government has actively promoted function-based reform with the aim of improving the management systems of these institutions. Such museums have a steady source of funding for wages, basic operating costs, as well as limited special funds for projects. This kind of financial policy has transported these "public museums" back to the system of state-supported institutions, which dates back before the era of Reform; they enjoy a relatively carefree existence.

This is great progress. In the post-Reform era, museums were seen as units of production that did not produce profits; they were seen as a burden on the government and were forced to survive on their own self-generated revenues. In the early days of the Reform and Opening-Up, many state-owned enterprises faced bankruptcy, unable to adapt to these economic changes. Therefore, some museums became self-supporting and were managed by travel agencies, or they assumed a lesser fate as souvenir shops.

The survival of most museums at that time relied on space rental, and some museums at the district and county levels had to sell their cultural resources, old goods, even relics such as stone rubbings, in order to survive. Of course, some museums successfully found a way out of this conundrum through good management or their own existing resources.

In recent years, "public museums" that enjoy full public financial subsidies are free from this struggle, but this funding comes with strings attached. Any income earned by the museum is returned to the central government and cannot be distributed to employees in the form of a bonus. As a result, the management of these museums have limited mechanisms to motivate employee performance. Although salaries increase year by year according to national regulations, there are limited options for performance bonuses. For instance, some policies stipulate that all products developed and produced with central government funds cannot be sold. Thus, a large number of catalogs gather dust in storage, their cultural and economic value left untapped.

In 2016, the Chinese government took steps to balance relics and public when the National People's Congress (NPC) passed a law, the Guarantee of Cultural Public Service, which provides a legal basis for the construction, operation, standards of service, funding sources, management methods, assessment, and evaluations within the museum sector. Therefore, this law provides a solid legal basis for the development of a unified museum standard and the realization of common goals and social responsibilities of museums.

With the continuous development of these reforms, the various confusions and contradictions faced by Chinese museums will gradually be resolved. Diverse funding sources will eventually be established, and the modern corporate governance system will bring museum management to a new level—one that is focused on the entirety of the museum's functions.

PART II:
MUSEUM BUILDING IN CHINA'S NEW URBAN CULTURE

12 Shanghai city model at the Shanghai Urban Planning Exhibition Center (2000).
Photography: Rebecca Catching

7

THE URBAN BOOM MEETS MUSEUMS

Doug Saunders

China's museum boom cannot be understood without an appreciation of the unique role China's cities have played during the last two decades. The construction of museums as focal points in hundreds of cities is not just an inevitable consequence of the unprecedented pace and scope of China's urban growth; it is also a result of the specific ways in which Chinese municipalities govern themselves, expand their populations, make use of land, raise revenues, organize their living spaces and communities, plan major projects, and attempt to create civic space and economic activity. All of this happens against the backdrop of competition with other cities for investment, migration, visitors, and civic recognition.

To outsiders, China is most often seen as a highly centralized, centrally-planned superpower overseen by a national, authoritarian government centered in Beijing. In day-to-day practice, however, Chinese are governed by hundreds of municipal entities, each with its own distinct practices, local laws, fiscal structures and hierarchies, cultural expressions, and planning agendas. Each of these entities is autonomous within parameters broadly established by the national government. This new structure, composed of a network of cities, is a recent development, emerging after the economic liberalization of the 1980s as part of the explosion of urban life in China. It took its full form in the late 1990s and early 2000s, as city governments replaced work units and agricultural collectives as the crucial nodes of Chinese life. China is not just a country containing hundreds of major cities—since the turn of this century, those cities have become the essence of the country itself.

It has, during the past decade, become almost mandatory for Chinese cities with more than a million inhab-

itants to commission a famous international architect to design a landmark building that will serve as a civic focal point—a hall, center, or museum, or some combination—in an effort to identify or "brand" the city, both internationally and for the benefit of its own residents, the way Sydney did with its opera house or Bilbao did with the Guggenheim. At their best (and there are many splendid designs), these new facilities are woven into the urban fabric to create intimate public spaces that *really do* improve urban life. Others are examples of excellent architecture but not necessarily of great urbanism: they are often surrounded by parking or parade-square space, or isolated on an isthmus or roadway-interchange space. They create an urban skyline without weaving an urban fabric. Some are beautiful buildings in search of an identity—some sense of their audience, content, or public function. While there is a sophisticated understanding of urban theory among China's urban scholars, planners, and some developers, they often have trouble translating theory into practice when executed by officials who place a priority on automobile-led transportation, security, and lucrative property deals.

This institution-building drive, with its multiple and complex motives, has dovetailed with a genuine desire in Chinese cities to develop a sense of coherence, cultural unity, and history. The last decade has seen a rise in nostalgia for the more intimate, human-scale cities of the 20th century and a greater appreciation of pre-socialist patterns of urban life. The alleyways and courtyards of Beijing's old residential *hutong* districts and Shanghai's labyrinthine *shikumen* neighborhoods, with their dense patchwork of low-lying houses and intimate spaces, were denigrated and rejected for decades as unmodern and unhygienic, and most were demolished. Today they are

Figure 13 The Jing'an sculpture park surrounding the Shanghai Natural History Museum (1956, 2015) provides open space for free-play and imagination in a dense urban environment. *Photography: Rebecca Catching*

Figure 14 The Chengdu Museum (2016, Sichuan), by Sutherland Hussey Harris. *Photography: Lai Jin Xiao Cangshu Ba*

often venerated, prized by well-off urban hipsters who purchase and renovate them and carefully preserved in heritage sites such as Shanghai's Shikumen Open House Museum, the coastal Chinese counterpart to New York City's Tenement Museum. There are municipal battles over whether to preserve or modernize the old winding, unplanned working-class and migrant districts of cities such as Tianjin and Shenzhen. The solution is often to rebuild the district in a sanitized replica of its former self—labeled a "historic culture street," often with modern shopping and other amenities. There is also a genuine urban cultural-preservation movement that is developing a stronger voice—and a real market emerging for more traditionally "urbanist" housing. China's urban spaces are overwhelmingly ahistorical—both by design and by circumstance (most appeared only very recently). Chinese urbanites, seeking the sort of deep-rooted ties their parents and grandparents had to their villages, are seeking a sense of continuity, connection, and importance, a historical narrative in which to situate their own lives.

This combination of a civic sense of architectural monumentalism and a growing public sense of historical and artistic relevance is transforming the landscape and atmosphere of hundreds of Chinese cities. Museums such as the Chengdu Museum by Sutherland Hussey Harris, the Design Society by Fumihiko Maki, the new National Art Museum of China by MAD Architects, the Fishing Culture Center and Museum in Hainan, and the Taiyuan Museum of Art by Preston Scott Cohen are evidence of this trend.

Building Cities from Villages

To understand how this surprising museum-building urge has materialized, we need to examine the people, policies, geographies, and economies that have shaped China's urban explosion. If Mao Zedong infamously ordered that "the countryside should surround the cities, and finally seize them," that equation has been reversed during this century. The cities have not only absorbed the village, regulating the movement of its residents, but they have consumed it as their raw material for growth. China may today contain 129 cities with more than a million inhabitants, but it cannot be understood without appreciating how tightly connected those cities are to the villages and to the village life that formed the core of the Chinese experience only a generation ago.

"We are a nation of villagers who happen to live in big cities."

This sentiment, in various forms, has become commonplace in Chinese dialogue; I've heard it expressed by dozens of people across China from all walks of life, and it is a central motif in current works of Chinese literature such as Xiong Peiyun's highly popular nonfiction work *My Village, My Country*. That sentiment is key to understanding the peculiar nature of the modern Chinese city and the explosion of cultural institutions it has created. "Villagers who happen to live in cities" has three important meanings.

First, it means that China's urban growth has been so rapid, and so recent, that virtually every urban Chinese family has recent memories of living close to the land.

Although it has had a sophisticated administrative and political system and been technologically advanced for millennia, China has not historically been an urban nation. The cities of imperial China mainly served as administrative centers until the late 19th century, when its tragic military encounters with British imperialism saw the development of big trading cities, such as the treaty ports of the Pearl and Yangtze River Deltas.

Under state socialism after 1949, the growth of China's cities was deliberately restricted—at first cautiously, under policies in the 1950s and early 1960s that sharply restricted migration to cities, employing them strictly as centers of industrial production (which conversely, restricted villages strictly to agriculture). For the decade and a half of the Cultural Revolution, China was purposefully and systematically deurbanized: tens of millions of urbanites were forcibly moved into collectivized peasant villages for reeducation; cities were de-invested, stripped of their financial resources, and left to decay and to depopulate.

It was not until the early 1980s that China's cities really began to grow again—at first gradually, as a cautious experiment, and then, a decade later, explosively. Premier Deng Xiaoping began opening up certain cities to profit-seeking business development under Township and Village Enterprise (TVE) initiatives, which allowed industrial production and investment to return to smaller centers, and a set of experimental Special Economic Zones—larger urban areas that permitted capitalist production, along with land leasing and some forms of taxation. The most famous, and earliest, of these, was Shenzhen, which in 1979 was a small market-and-fishing town of fewer than 30,000 people across from Hong Kong that changed almost overnight into a manufacturing, technology, and trade city of millions.

As the 1990s progressed, countless more Special Economic Zones and similar non-collective territories were created, including Shantou, Zhuhai, Hainan, Xiamen, and Pudong (Shanghai). By the early 2000s, Chinese cities were market-driven places competing for investment, business, and workers, and the country's entire organizational structure and ethos had become urban in nature.

The result was the largest and the most rapid shift in human population in the planet's history. China's 1982 census found that 20.6 percent of its billion citizens lived in cities—in 2010, the urban proportion of China's 1.4-billion population passed 50 percent—a percentage achieved by the world in 2008 and by the United Kingdom at the turn of the century, with other Western countries urbanizing in the following decades. Yet most Chinese families are new to the city, and that sense of recent arrival has a significant impact on urban culture and policy.

Second, it means that a large proportion of China's city-dwellers are, legally and officially, still villagers—and the growth, culture, and ambitions of Chinese cities are shaped in many ways by this huge "floating population."

For six decades, the lives of most Chinese citizens have been circumscribed by their *hukou* or "household-registration permit," which registers families, more or less permanently, as rural or urban, and as residents of a specific village or city. Officially, families may only receive housing, social services, and education in the city or town where they are registered. This policy was implemented to stop the flow of migration from rural areas to cities. Even after living somewhere else for years, and sometimes for generations, a rural family's *hukou* does not change.

The result is a truly enormous "floating population" of Chinese urbanites. The 2010 census counted 221 million of these "migrants."

It was apparent to authorities, from the early 2000s onward, that this huge unofficial population of long-term urban residents who have no access to public services was creating large-scale social and economic problems. On the rural end, China has become home to hundreds of millions of children growing up in "hollow villages" populated only by children being raised and schooled by their grandparents; the entire adult population has moved to the city. The urban phenomena are equally dramatic. Sometimes these rural-urban migrants build their own urban neighborhoods upon marginal or unclaimed land, creating "villages" within the city with their own substantial internal economies and self-provided services (I document one such neighborhood in Chongqing in my book *Arrival City*). In other cases, these villagers settle in expensive market-rental accommodations and struggle to pay for private versions of public services. Central Beijing is home to a substantial population known as "ant people"—families renting windowless rooms in basement or sub-basement quarters of buildings; many are well-educated lower-middle-class rural people who find themselves forced into these stygian quarters in order to afford private-school fees for their children.

In an attempt to remedy this, the last decade has seen waves of reforms designed to make it somewhat easier for villagers employed in the city to apply for urban *hukou*; in 2016, the Ministry of Public Security announced that it had issued 28.9 million new urban residency permits under new rules. But many of the largest and most economically successful cities, concerned about population growth (Beijing, Shanghai, Guangzhou, Shenzhen, Chengdu, Wuhan, and Xi'an) have imposed tougher rules based on a "points system" that allows residents to gain urban *hukou* only if they can prove high levels of education, proof of tax payment, and work experience. The government announced in 2017 that it plans to issue urban *hukou* to 100 million people by 2020. But because the new rules force "migrant workers" to relinquish their rural land tenure immediately, and because the urban housing market is so expensive and difficult to enter, there is considerable doubt as to whether this target can be met.

The long-term ambiguous status of this "floating population" has shaped the culture and development of China's cities. These residents from faraway villages are often viewed by more established urbanites as alien and unwelcome, much as international immigrants are viewed elsewhere. This struggle for urban legitimacy has been the defining drama of Chinese urban life in the 21st century and has created two distinct layers of urban life and culture, one for the legally urban and another for those who must remain tied to an often-distant village, which has implications for both civic pride and the sense of ownership of cultural institutions.

Third, it means that China's cities have grown and prospered by enveloping villages and using rural land as their key source of income and growth. In essence, many Chinese cities have only been able to sustain themselves by absorbing rural land—by very physically becoming a city of villages.

Because China developed historically as an overwhelmingly rural country, it did not traditionally have a history of incorporated, independent cities with taxation and revenue-raising abilities—in the 20th century, cities were fiscally dependent on the national government. This became a problem when China's authorities began pursuing urban-led industrial growth in the 1980s, and cities found themselves expanding fast while lacking any real structures of municipal governance or finance. At first, the only significant source of revenue to pay for infrastructure and services was the sale of public and collectivized rural land

for development. Collective farms were (and still are) often turned into urban development land by giving the farmers urban *hukou*, public-housing apartments, and some social service benefits in exchange for the privatization and development of their fields. In 2004, for example, Shenzhen gained 235 square kilometers of land by reclassifying villagers as urbanites and abolishing their collectives.

In 1998, China's constitution was amended to allow land to be used as a commodity ("the right to land use may be transferred")—effectively allowing cities to lease land and sell land-use rights, with leases lasting up to 50 years for commercial use. This almost immediately became the main source of municipal revenue, as both foreign and Chinese companies and housing developers rushed to lease land or to finance large-scale infrastructure projects in exchange for land-use rights.

"Local governments acquire land cheaply from peasants and leverage it to attract business and investment," writes the urban-development scholar Yuan Xiao in her description of the "land grab" financing of Chinese cities. "However, [this practice] has become increasingly unsustainable because of the huge inequality, intense social conflicts, and economic inefficiency it has created. The central government of China has issued strict policy measures to curb land conversion by local governments. In response, a new institution has emerged—the land quota market. These markets are developed by local governments to trade 'land development quotas. . . .'" Quotas are created by tearing down low-density farmhouses and packing peasants into high-rise apartments. The development rights of old parcels are then sold in a market. This new quota market has changed the calculus of land values: instead of location advantage, land value is more dependent on the spatial density of existing farmhouses so that even land in the hinterlands is affected by urbanization.

Local governments use these land-leasing practices to finance improvements in infrastructure; this, in turn, opens up more and more land on the urban periphery to development—a cycle that then repeats itself, over and over, as infrastructure-investment deals and land-leasing deals become mutually reinforcing (and mutually enriching) poles of urban growth.

Chinese city officials are duly aware of the built-in problem with this form of urban finance: that it depends entirely on continuous urban growth. If Chinese cities stop physically expanding, they die economically.

Starting at the end of the first decade of the 21st century, larger Chinese cities began to respond to this problem by experimenting with property taxes—levied at first on more expensive properties, then more widely. At the end of 2017, finance minister Xiao Jie announced plans to develop a nationwide, municipally administered property-tax system, starting with the creation of a property-value registry in 2019. This novel development has led to new forms of activism in which groups of homeowners, expecting government services and responses in return for the taxes they've paid, have organized protests, reform movements, and politicized homeowners' associations. Taxation, in other words, is creating a popular demand for representation—at least on the municipal level.

A shift to tax-based finance could change the growth dynamics of China's cities. Their three-decade explosion was essentially a wholesale occupation of space—by transport infrastructure, by housing, by industrial and office space, and of course by hundreds of millions of people. Every few years Beijing added a new ring road, and thus another effective city-within-a-city. Shenzhen has enveloped the farmlands that had been its identity. Shanghai has turned former null spaces and quiet markets into gleaming commercial districts, and Wuhan, Hangzhou, Changzhou, and Nanjing have crept along both banks of the Yangtze, turning much of the great river into a continuous urban belt. The shift to tax-based finance is part of a slow recognition, across China, that the big cities have grown outward enough, and that it is now time to focus on the internal growth, to turn these places of architectural and human sprawl into unified wholes.

Cities Seeking a Center

These three factors—the extraordinary newness of most Chinese urban space, the rootlessness of much of the urban population, and the need for cities to expand constantly across rural land—have combined to produce an identity crisis. Urban residents and officials have spoken, since the late 1990s, of a lack of a sense of belonging, an absence of municipal history or culture, an inability to find the symbolic or physical center, an aimless sameness to the urban form—a feeling, to borrow Gertrude Stein's description of the fast-urbanizing California of the last century, that "there is no there there."

This absence of urban-identity focal points is partly because of the nature of Chinese urban growth; it is also because of the distinctive organization of Chinese cities. Most Chinese urban families live in *xiaoqu*—usually translated as "housing area" or "residential compound." These are generally enclosed neighborhoods—until the end of the 1990s, predominantly worker-dormitory compounds attached to factories, but today also apartment or housing districts. Some are even "gated communities" (in the Western sense). A *xiaoqu* typically is built around a central park, where residents exercise, relax, and meet together; it has its own school and shops; its own community gov-

ernance, of one form or another; and it is, to a greater or lesser degree, gated and guarded. The *xiaoqu* system often gives Chinese urbanites a sense of community coherence that would be enviable in other countries, but it can make cities themselves atomized, uncentered, and hard to navigate. Many cities, until recently, were little more than huge sprawling collections of *xiaoqu* with factories, and an urban center devoted to governance and service provision. The city composed solely of *xiaoqu* contains too many barriers for working-class residents entering the middle class. The system tends to preserve socioeconomic status rather than offering pathways to higher levels of employment or entrepreneurship and makes it difficult for cities to differentiate themselves and bring residents together politically and culturally.

Bring in the Museums

For cities themselves (that is, for the party officials and administrators who run them, and for the business, community, and cultural groups that dominate them), this lack of a "center" has become the crucial challenge in development, planning, and expenditure. With their newfound wealth from land-leasing and development deals, cities large and small have increasingly been engaging in what urbanists call "place-making"—the creation of symbolic, public, and official spaces that give cities both a sense of place and a reason to attract people. The museum boom is in part a consequence of this impulse.

The big infrastructure investments of the early years of Chinese urban growth were all nuts-and-bolts projects: superhighways, elaborate subway networks, high-speed rail lines, tunnels, airports, shipping ports, and big public squares and stadiums devoted to a celebration of the Party, which often felt the same as those in other cities. What cities found themselves lacking was fourfold: first, the sort of infrastructure, institutions, and spaces that felt unique and were symbolic of the city's identity; second, a genuine center, historic or otherwise, that would draw people together; third, institutions and spaces that would give residents a sense of belonging and togetherness; and fourth (often seen as most fiscally important), anything that would enable the city to differentiate itself competitively—like the skylines of Shanghai or Hong Kong, or the lakes and canals of Hangzhou and Suzhou—or a quality of life or a set of cultural attractions that would give the city an advantage over hundreds of other Chinese urban spaces in attracting important foreign and domestic corporations, educated middle-class residents, and attention on the international stage.

This urgent need for a sense of "place" and centrality has combined with Xi Jinping's demand for middle-class growth and the infrastructure-spending boom to create an enormous market in symbolic, monumental, and culturally emblematic architecture, institutions, and urban features—of which the boom in museums (along with opera houses, convention centers, stadiums, and elite shopping centers, often in the same, architecturally distinctive space) is a significant and visible part. The urbanist Xuefei Ren, in her study of urban China, describes the economic forces behind this uncontrollable spiral of institution-building:

> The spending on fixed-asset investment—a measure that captures building activities such as real estate and infrastructure construction, among other things—has reached an alarming 70 percent of the national GDP, and infrastructure spending has passed foreign trade as the biggest contributor to national economic growth.[4]

She asserts that this overspending has caused municipal governments to incur large debts due to the way that political performance has traditionally been tied to real estate and infrastructure. The fiscal and political forces that have provoked an explosion of monumental public and private structures have coincided with a civic and popular drive to create urban places with a center and a past. Together, these factors have created a mass appetite for heritage and history that did not previously exist, along with a need to create attractive public spaces and institutions that can make the Chinese city whole and make it a desirable destination for newcomers and visitors. The hundreds of millions of new residents of Chinese cities, most of whom now have some sort of ownership stake, through property ownership or tax participation, in their city's growth and development, do not want to live in places known mainly for sprawl, air pollution, and traffic congestion. There is a strong sense of urban pride—and interurban competitiveness—among the new, urban-born generation of Chinese city-dwellers. If the explosive growth and uniquely lucrative financing of Chinese cities has given rise to an almost immeasurable glut of cultural institutions, there is equally a huge and fast-growing population of urban residents with a strong desire to imbue those institutions with genuine content and meaning. The next decade of urban growth is more likely to point inward, in a mass quest to turn these impressive new structures into meaningful expressions of China's new urban life.

Doug Saunders

8

A MUSEUM BORN OF REAL ESTATE

Gao Peng

In 2014, the Today Art Museum held a special event to celebrate Valentine's Day and Chinese New Year, which happened to coincide that year. The event was titled "Today We Hug" and was a participatory event that asked visitors to participate in a "hugging performance," to bring a friend, a family member, or partner to the museum and maintain an unbroken hug for 13 minutes and 14 seconds. Numbers 1, 3, 1, 4 (yi san yi si), when said in succession, sound like the phrase "yi sheng yi she" 一生一世 meaning throughout one's life.

Hugging is not as common in China as it is in the West, so it was interesting to watch people's reactions. During the event, I noticed a father trying to hold his daughter, but twice she broke away, feeling awkward and embarrassed. He tried to hug her a third time, and they clung together for the remainder of the time. After they parted, the father said to his daughter: "The day will soon come when you'll grow up and get married. . . . But you know what? Dad really wants to hold you for as long as I can, in the same way as I held you when you were a baby."

I chose to mention this event not only to highlight the sometimes provocative programming—which asks the viewer to think deeply about their relationships, creating memories at the same time—but also to serve as a metaphor for the public's relationship to contemporary art, one that though awkward at its inception has the capacity to become profound and long-lasting.

As one of the first private museums of art in China, founded in Beijing in 2002, Today Art Museum has seen the full arc of this relationship. When we first opened, contemporary art had a fairly minimal following. People of my parents' generation typically find contemporary

art distasteful, preferring traditional landscape paintings or oil paintings of elegant women. That's to say nothing of performance art, which is quite misunderstood, seen as "weird characters running naked in the street." But today there has been a pretty radical transformation in the tastes of the public. The Museum features sculptures by Yue Minjun in our courtyard, which people thought pretty ugly at first. Now a lot of people stop and take pictures in front of them and have lots of fashion magazines come to the museum to shoot. They like the space and the contemporary atmosphere. Couples take wedding pictures in the 798 Art District as well as in the Today Art Museum. Unlike many state museums, which tend to have either historical buildings or gleaming new constructions, the Today Art Museum repurposed the existing architecture, the boiler room of a brewery. The architect Wang Hui made its repurposing purposely visible, by filling in the windows with bricks of a different color, to create a dialogue with the industrial heritage of the area. This use of industrial relics is also seen in 798, and later on in other private and public art museums such as the Power Station of Art and the Long Museum West Bund (both in Shanghai).

The history of the museum itself, in some ways, reflects this growing acceptance of contemporary art. Up until 2006, when the museum's first external director was appointed, the institution did not have a clear focus on contemporary art. Following his appointment, the museum began to focus more solidly on contemporary artists, developing a reputation for large solo shows by important contemporary masters, including Zhou Chunya, Yue Minjun, and Fang Lijun. Having secured the museum's positioning, the director then applied for nonprofit status for the museum, which made it the first nonprofit museum in China. The Today Art Museum was unique in two ways:

first in that it was one of the few contemporary art museums at the time (even today as few as 2 percent of Chinese museums are dedicated to contemporary art), and also in being a nonprofit museum, thus clearing the trail for other institutions to come. To use a Chinese expression, we were "feeling the stones as we crossed the river," since there were no previously existing models to learn from. Ten years on and the museum is still alive and continuing to evolve, building sustainable financial strategies, improving the efficiency of operations and building up the academic rigor of our exhibitions and publications.

With an area of 20,000 square meters, including three independent and complete exhibition halls; an exhibition space of 7,000 square meters; 300,000 to 500,000 visitors; and 30 independently organized exhibitions every year, the Today Art Museum is a thriving contemporary art institution.

Museum Background

Like many private museums, the Today Art Museum was born of the real estate industry; but now, though granted use of the land and the building free of charge, the museum operates as an independent entity. From 2002 to 2006, the owner of the real estate company was basically the director of the museum, but after obtaining its official nonprofit status, the museum chose an independent director to lead the museum team, raise funds, and plan exhibitions. In 2013, the Today Art Museum officially established its own foundation, further clarifying the system, so that the museum is led by a board of trustees that includes international members such as Dr. John Harris, head of the Birmingham School of Art; Jinsuk Suh, director of the Nam Jun Paik Art Center in South Korea; and prominent Chinese artist Wang Guanyi. Therefore, it is also the first private art museum in China that has established a complete foundation system and is independently operated by a professional director. This was significant in that it first acted as a test case for nonprofit organizations, and second, helped publicize its existence to the public, investors, and real estate developers, who until recently had only been familiar with corporate or governmental entities.

Given the arm's-length relationship to its backers, the museum relies heavily on sponsorship with internationally recognized brands and social and cultural organizations. The annual reports of the museum, which include the year's projects and income, can be freely downloaded by the public, thus providing an unprecedented level of transparency. Besides creating an open culture of museums, this also encourages more corporate sponsors to willingly support or donate to nonprofit cultural institutions, including art museums.

The modes of operation of private art museums in China are quite different from those of the West. There are many problems that are unique to China, which does not really have a tradition of corporate sponsorship. Beyond the question of how companies can donate to museums, there is the deeper question of *why they should* donate to museums. The situation has improved somewhat recently with the introduction of tax breaks, due to changes in national laws. The museum has also learned how to harness the power of its board (boards of trustees are also a relatively recent phenomenon in China).

A key strategy is to invite members of the boards of other museums who are very active internationally, who might be on the board of the Tate or other important institutions abroad, to extend the museum's reach and connections. The museum also adopted a systematic sponsorship system that delineates between key sponsors, equipment sponsors, strategic partners, media partners, and hotel and restaurant partners. Many sponsors not only sponsor works or projects but also sign three-year contracts with the museum—it is up to the museum's discretion to decide where and how to use the money, which provides more flexibility.

Beyond sponsorship of equipment and materials, the museum works closely with international cultural funding bodies including the British Council, the Goethe-Institut, Japan Foundation, Alliance Française, and the Cervantes Institute.

Creating Academic Credibility

As a private art museum, the most important thing is to build a reputation for academic rigor. In addition to collecting important modern and contemporary works of art, the museum pays special attention to the quality of its temporary exhibitions, much like a kunsthalle (in fact, many contemporary art museums in China follow a kunsthalle model). Since it is in the process of building a permanent collection, the museum has quite a bit of freedom to work almost exclusively with independent curators in order to maintain a sense of vitality and variety. The Today Art Museum was the first contemporary art museum in China to embrace sound art, using sound to explore various concepts related to Chinese philosophy and aesthetics. As such, we have developed a reputation in the Beijing community as a place where surprising things are bound to happen.

Another important facet of our academic branding is the "Future Pavilion," which aims to explore China's rapid economic development, culture, and technology, and finally the cultural aesthetics and exhibition-viewing habits of China's millennials, which are completely different from those of previous generations.

Figure 15 "Future of Today" exhibition at Today Art Museum (2002, Beijing) featuring the installation "Motion/Tension" by sculptor Sui Jianguo. The steel balls roll around the exhibition hall, creating a deafening sound that curator Wu Hung likens to the soundtrack of a construction site. *Photo courtesy: Today Art Museum*

The project aims to explore three different questions:

"What does the future of art museums look like?"

"What kind of art forms should future art museums present to the public?"

"What kind of interaction will future audiences require?"

Future Pavilion projects run on consecutive years, and the first round, which ran in 2015, explored the spatial elements of museums and consisted of three parts: a physical exhibition, a virtual exhibition, and a third-party augmented reality exhibition. In 2017, the second future pavilion, ".zip Future Rhapsody Xiaomi Future of Today," explored the concept of artistic digital space and immersive audience experiences. An experimental discussion of physical art museums, virtual reality, and future art forms, it reflects a profound exploration of the future of art and humanity. The project has also produced unique products based on the

exhibition concepts, which were distributed in New York, Chengdu, Dalian, Sanya, Wuhan, and other cities.

In its work, the museum tries to pursue a holistic path to development with exhibitions, academic research, art education, collections, the publication of books and magazines, and the artnow.com.cn website—a digital art museum platform, focusing on the gathering of digital materials as part of the collecting process.

Looking back on the development of Chinese contemporary art museums in the past decades, many museums fall into the same patterns and thus become indistinguishable, suffering from a lack of personality, which leads to a monoculture rather than a diverse museum ecology. To counter this, art museums should determine their own positioning and goals according to their own audience groups and communities, collections, and histories, building long-lasting relationships with these groups, no matter how awkward or difficult the first encounter might be.

9

FROM DENSIFICATION TO PLACE-MAKING IN URBAN PLANNING

Phil Enquist

When I started planning Chinese cities in 1994, I began in Shenzhen, working in conjunction with the local planning bureau. At that time, there was little talk of emphasizing culture, or defining the local art scenes or the creation of museums. The focus and goal for our young planning team was density, efficiency development strategies, sale of land, public access, and, most importantly, bringing these projects speedily to market. Far more emphasis was placed on the buildings and volume of needed space with little concern about what was inside these soon-to-be-constructed buildings or the kind of community they would eventually accommodate. Housing and work environments were the key; cultural initiatives were less important.

Even though the Shenzhen Planning Bureau was charged with the goals of achieving needed space, we were able to reach an agreement to create two new public parks, a pedestrian street, a restaurant "row" that connected the district into the adjacent city, and mixed strategies of housing, retail, and office in introducing planning practices that were new to Shenzhen at the time. Above all, we placed an emphasis on the ground floor of buildings that belonged to the community and to the life of the street—elements that are indigenous to many Chinese cities but are often ignored in contemporary urban planning. These planning principles were quickly understood, embraced, and implemented.

Through this process, we realized that achieving quality urban communities was a shared goal between our team and the planning bureau leaders; we were all in this together, moving quickly but carefully. We communicated the need for culture and open space, the need for respecting history and for creating a unique solution appropriate to Shenzhen, and our client group was listening. From the very begin-

ning of our work in China, we were committed to creating unique places, rather than cutting and pasting the same urban fabric from place to place, and I felt the government bureaus had similar commitments. In the last fifteen years, Shenzhen has since established itself as a major center of contemporary culture, and the city's identity, attractiveness, and economy have strengthened due to this broader cultural commitment. Shenzhen stands out as a model of culture, and museums play a key role in distinguishing a city.

Ever since the 1990s, Chinese cities have been facing intense pressure to accommodate urban migration from rural areas, using urban migration and city building as a way to address poverty, accommodate new industries, and at the same time, create innovative 21st-century urban environments that can compete on the global stage.

From Shenzhen, our team quickly expanded to Tianjin, Shanghai, Beijing, Nanjing, Wuhan, Xi'an, and other first- and second-tier cities. We worked with urban planning bureaus to give them the framework for future decision making in terms of the best ways to create vibrant urban districts. We prioritized local geography, identity, open space, ecology, and preservation of built places in terms of where new building growth should occur. But to be honest, museums and cultural amenities were not seen as influencers of city planning. At the scale we were working, the museums were simply another land use to plan for in some way, and not seen as an essential asset.

The Shift from Density to Uniqueness

The emphasis in city planning within China has shifted over the last decade from prioritizing density, speed, and

Figure 16 Shanghai's Urban Planning Exhibition Hall (2001) draws crowds of visitors to view the Shanghai City Model. *Photography: Rebecca Catching*

volume of built space to uniqueness of place, cultural investments, effective transit strategies, and ecological sustainability. We have seen a remarkable shift in government priorities and also in the collaborative efforts between private and public initiatives in building urban districts and cultural infrastructure. Not all land is seen as "for development," and the ecological and cultural framework of communities has become a strong influencing factor.

As urban planners, we experienced a growing emphasis on providing venues for local culture and heritage and nurturing a stronger art ecology throughout China as a means to highlight uniqueness and celebrate local history and traditions. I think this awakening has come about with the realization that the nation has bulldozed away the texture of their culture and history throughout this 30-year development sprint.

It is now accepted that culture can create economies, can be utilized to bridge new growth with existing communities, can connect international tourism and business with local communities, and attract and retain talent. China's cities and urban districts have the ability to engage culture and education in a variety of ways, through environmental commitments, open space strategies, the arts, local traditions, and cultures.

As urban planning made the shift from density to uniqueness, museums in China have exploded from just a few to many thousands, both private and public. If there is ever a place to reinvent the concept of the museum and how people engage with these institutions, it is China. Many of the most impressive museums are dedicated to the arts and are identified by remarkable architecture. However, we have come across some museums, especially the smaller museums, that are focused on local culture, unique place, history, food, and local industries that provide impressive value for visitors but also seem to touch on education and local community involvement. The inherent power of museums lies in their roles as "bridges" between local and global, between various industries and arts, between history and future.

The Power of Site-Specific Museums

One of the most charming and interesting museums for me is in Wuxi—a very fast-growing city in Jiangsu

Province near Suzhou. The Wuxi Ancient Kiln Cluster Museum, located at the intersection of the Bodugang and the Jinhang canals in the historic city, displays the rich brick- and tile-making culture that once existed in Wuxi. The museum tells stories of the extraction of clay, the forming of bricks and tiles, the growing and harvesting of the local fuel sources from the fields, the art of firing, and the logistics of transporting these high-quality objects through intricate canal systems to the various cities and palaces. It is a site-specific museum that could not exist in any other place.

The Kiln Museum is an unexpected cultural and historic experience, set in a complex of historic buildings, that is unique in the world and helps a visitor understand what drove the Wuxi industries and economies of centuries past. I found it not only refreshing and unique, but it helped me understand why this city is a special place within China. It bridges history with the future of the city's growth; it explains the city's canal systems, the importance of local agriculture, and the uniqueness of this craftsmanship. The small and intimate museum attracts a rich mix of local and national Chinese tourists as well as international tourists. The building complex does not stand alone as an architectural monument but rather integrates beautifully into the historic canal district.

This sense of place is an important part of our practice. For instance, we are currently working in the City of Jinan, the capital of the Shandong Province best known for its freshwater natural springs. In the heart of Jinan's new central business district, we were able to convince the city government to preserve the architecture of the large-scale steel mills to be repurposed to house emerging cultural institutions and community educational programs. This industrial architecture became the centerpiece of this new district. The project is now underway, and our aim is that the cultural landmark in the heart of Jinan will contribute to a unique identity. The Jinan city leaders saw this addition of a cultural venue in an industrial building as a long-term value added for their central business district investments.

Museums and Culture as Catalysts for Generating Unique District Identities

In the northeast corner of Beijing, near Wangjing, the 798 Art District is one of the more interesting examples of how local cultural assets can be used to generate a sense of place. The arts community was housed in a cluster of decommissioned factory buildings—the site of a former munitions factory built in 1957. In 1995, the Central Academy of Fine Art used the space as a temporary studio for its students, and slowly a trickle of artists began to move in. Today 798 is a thriving creative cluster featuring interna-

tionally renowned museums and galleries, gift shops, and restaurants—a major magnet for local and international tourism. As rents in 798 rose, many artists moved out to the "urban villages" surrounding 798, such as Heiqiaocun, Feijiacun, and also Caochangdi—the latter being home to many local and international galleries. Sadly, these communities were not considered worthy of preservation. As 798 illustrates, when these creative communities are allowed to take root and thrive, they can become engines of economic activity that help build the character of the region. The presence of this grassroots district, built organically from bottom up, can provide rich added value to the district as a whole, becoming a bridge between local and global, past and future.

The Great "Pre-Boom" Museum and Its Influence

We have worked for years with the Xi'an government in urban planning and the development of the new western districts of this historic city. The Xi'an district of Yanta, one of the nine major districts within Xi'an, has benefited greatly from the presence of the great Shaanxi History Museum. The museum is definitely a bridge between the local and national tourism destinations within this city. The Yanta urban district is a cultural hub of new public spaces, walkable districts, a mix of hotels, commercial, housing, and workplaces. The center of gravity of this district is the museum itself.

Historic Districts and Cultural Programming

In the historic city of Weishan, near Dali in Yunnan Province, we were able to preserve the historic core of the city and create cultural programs around the historic district. We managed to preserve a great collection of historic courtyard houses as well as traditional businesses and redirect new growth to areas so as to prevent damage to the buildings in the historic district.

In Kunming, the capital city of the Yunnan Province in southwestern China, we have been able to collaborate with the city to create a great park system at the abandoned inner-city airport. The park tried to address the city's ecological problems, including algae blooms and poor water quality. This new wetland park is proposed to house extensive cultural facilities for Kunming and was influenced by Chicago's Millennium Park. As well as playing a role to filter the city's freshwater resources, the future museums within this park will connect to the ecological needs of the city and the nation.

We had another opportunity to maximize sense of place with Chongming Island in the middle of the Yangtze River. On the island near Shanghai, we were able to emphasize food and farming as the primary industry to promote the protection of farmland and quality food production rather than follow the proposed plan for industrial development. Farming is a core business of the Island, and during the Great Cultural Revolution there were a number of projects to create the farming infrastructure of canals and levees. The new public wetland gardens in Chongming emphasize river habitat, bird migration, and local arts. These are just some of the encouraging success stories, where historic districts, ecological, and agricultural regions are preserved, while at the same time promoting culture and expanding access to education.

Today many people say that in the last 30 years, China has made all its cities look the same. However, there has been a growing recognition among Chinese urban planners and their foreign advisors like myself that leveraging local culture and global culture together with education and conscious, proactive place-making, can make cities and especially newly-planned urban districts more human, rooted, and ultimately more interesting. In the global and local art and design scenes, the historical qualities of a community are increasingly being celebrated and leveraged to create a unique sense of place, and some unforgettable experiences.

10

CHARACTER BUILDING AND GENIUS LOCI IN MUSEUM ARCHITECTURE

He Jingtang

Since cultural buildings are viewed as unique landmarks that house recognized public entities, they have always aroused the keen interest of architects. In recent years, due to our practice of integrating production, education, and research, our team at the South China University of Technology has been asked to design several different cultural facilities. Our portfolio includes many excellent designs (figure 10.1) that were underpinned by a certain subset of philosophies. We can categorize these ideas under the rubric of "Two Views and Three Characteristics."

Looking back, we could see clearly the underlying philosophies and values that characterized our approach to design. More specifically, these "two views" are first, a holistic view, and second, a view of sustainable growth. The three characteristics are locality, cultural orientation, and reflecting current trends or times.[1] These concepts, with their comprehensiveness and internal harmonies, provide answers to basic questions in architecture in a dialectical way and offer us guidance in our methodology that can be applied in design. To be exact, we need to explore the geographic environment and cultural traditions so as to find out what leads to the generation of space types and *genius loci*. With exploration, we can further enrich the cultural aspects of the design and increase the quality of the building to make it more culturally rich. Moreover, our designs incorporate the latest progress in such areas as art, technology, and materials. In this chapter, we will present our own design story and provide an analytical account of our experiences in designing cultural architecture.

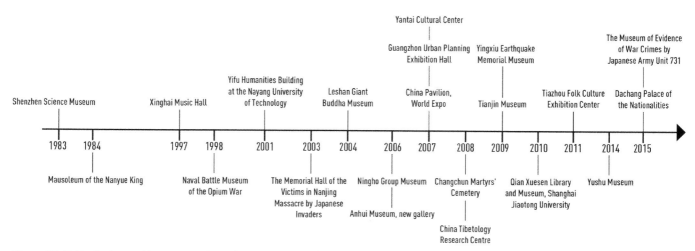

Figure 17 Table listing architecture projects for museums and cultural institutions created by the Architecture and Design School, South China University of Technology.

Figure 18 Wenchuan Earthquake Epicenter Yingxiu Memorial (2009) (left: view of site, right: the completed building).

Seeking Genius Loci

A building is built in a local context. It is located in a specific geographical environment and is exposed to the influence of such regional specificities as weather, landscape, and other geographical factors. Considering the local environment is a general rule for successful building design. But "geographical context" refers not just to the "regional features" mentioned above; it is more about the awareness of regional identity and the recognition of the local cultural traditions. To be specific, the expression of regional features in design goes beyond the techniques we use in general building design; it extends to localities closely related to building styles, which inject new cultural characteristics. As for the interpretation of the "DNA" of the locality and its reconstruction, we have drawn out the following seven principles.

Addressing Significant Events

This rule is often applied to memorials or institutions on sites where a significant event has occurred. In such cases, the buildings and places where these structures are located invariably are oriented toward a relatively clear "cultural character," which is closely related to the topic of the incident or event. For example, the memorial building we designed to commemorate a momentous natural disaster—the Wenchuan earthquake—is located at the epicenter in Yingxiu, outside of Chengdu. The building is framed around the "heaviness" of this event in the hope of showing multiple cultural traits within this "heaviness" and taking a holistic approach in the arrangement of the site layout. In an effort to achieve this goal, the whole building is integrated into the landscape from the ground view. Three significant lines highlight the outline of the whole building in a simple fashion, marking a profound sense of commemoration and delivering a sense of strength that was the dominant theme of that period. The thread of three themes, "collapse, reemergence, and hope," connects the three complexes, creating a complete narrative in a space where people can enjoy a rich emotional and intellectual experience of compassion and closure.

Recognizing the Limitations of the Site

In the design of cultural architecture, seemingly unfavorable conditions *can*, with the use of scientific analysis and smart applications of research, inspire unique personalized designs. For instance, some irregular layouts or spaces in the buildings might seem to appear without our being aware of them. These irregularities can be properly dealt with if the specific conditions of the site are taken into account.[2] A case in point is the expansion project of the Memorial Hall

Figure 19 The Memorial Hall of the Victims of the Nanjing Massacre (2003) by Japanese Invaders (expansion project).

He Jingtang

Figure 20 The Memorial Hall of the Victims of the Nanjing Massacre (2003) by Japanese Invaders commemorates the loss of over 300,000 civilians who were raped, tortured, and murdered by Japanese troops during December and January 1937. *Photography: Kevin Dooley*

of the Victims of the Nanjing Massacre by Japanese Invaders. First, the exaggerated and powerful triangular shape of the new complex comes from the inward squeezing of the outline of the façade. Secondly, in the expanded part, we adopted a structure that was "half visible, half invisible," that is to make half of this subtle slope stand out above the ground, and have the other half below ground, to place it in a humble position in regard to the existing premises. Metaphorically, this symbolizes the shape of a broken army knife buried in the soil. In addition, many walls are built to shield the site from its mundane urban surroundings, thus generating an aura of solemnity throughout the site.

Taking Cultural Traditions into Account

Cultural traditions in this context stand for both a recognition of the local culture and sometimes that of the folk culture. Different from earlier philosophies that previously guided design composition, current ideas behind the representation of local cultural traditions in contemporary cultural buildings emphasize a reflection of the times, through abstraction and simplicity.[3] A case in point is the design of the Tianjin Museum. Since ancient times, Tianjin has been a key logistics port, a transportation hub, and a window for communication. Interpreting these local specificities, the designer used "windows of the centuries" as the theme for the museum. The idea was expressed through the arrangement of public space that opened to the city through a huge window. In designing the Dachang Cultural Palace of the Nationalities, we embodied important facets of folk culture by integrating the Zhou dynasty philosophy of "dome-like heaven embraces the vast Earth," which has parallels with the characteristics of Islamic architecture, which we interpreted through an innovative and abstract lens. This project combined both Chinese and Islamic elements, being a space dedicated to China's Muslim minority groups, and included spaces for worship, a theater, and a community center.

Meeting Functional and Space Requirements

Responding to the potential needs of visitors, exhibition spaces and exhibition design

Cultural architecture differs from other types of buildings because first, it serves unique functions, and second, it is born with an obvious cultural character or cultural properties. For a building, such cultural character tends to be an ambiance created by both the shape of the building and the arrangement of space. The question of how to deal with and interpret such "cultural character" is one of the higher pursuits of architectural practice.

Understanding Culture in Architecture

Generally speaking, cultural property represents a "combination" of both the spirit and the ambiance of an abstract thing, based on its basic function and the concrete form. Yet we cannot understand a building's culture by considering it in isolation. By analyzing the inherent structure of the building's culture from the perspective of our philosophy of "Two Views and Three Characteristics," we discover that the cultural properties of a building are related to where the building is built. To be more specific, the locality, in fact, tells us something about the regional landscape and the legacy of the local cultural traditions. Our reflection and understanding of "time" include a contemplation of how time interacts with technology, art, and social progress. Therefore, the "Three Characteristics" are interrelated and indispensable to each other.

At the core of a superb work of architecture lie both a dialogue with the history of the area and a harmonious relationship with its natural surroundings. This kind of macroscopic and holistic view of the construction of culture requires us to be analytical and comprehensive, to contemplate individual elements and also the whole, to contemplate the contemporary and the traditional, and finally, to contemplate a larger perspective on time and space to carry out a general summary of the qualities and the characteristics of the architecture. That is to say, we need to define what characteristics influence the nature of architectural form from a wider perspective of "space-time." In other words, the cultural properties of a piece of architecture are created by the integration of a series of factors that include the building itself and its historical and geographical context.

Defining the Cultural Character of a Building

A building, like a human being, generally possesses a basic character, which results from a combination of factors.

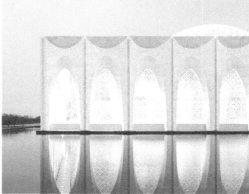

Figure 21 Left: Tianjin Museum (2009). Right: Dachang Cultural Palace of the Nationalities (2015).

Figure 22 Left: China Pavilion, Shanghai World Expo (2007). Right: Anhui Museum (2006).

We believe that it's important to explore the "roots" of the building's cultural character by paying attention to the regional environment. However, the richness of the concept of locality, e.g., where the building is located, makes it impossible for us to discern the basic pattern of how this cultural character manifests itself in architecture. Only by analyzing and synthesizing the concrete conditions of the situation can we have a complete and clear picture of the cultural character of the building to be built.

Let's take the design of the China Pavilion in the World Expo as an example. As the World Expo was a showcase of the latest achievements in human progress, its overall function required different cultures to gather and mingle. In designing the pavilion, we wanted to express the confidence of China as a great power on the rise. Moreover, we wanted the pavilion to embody a unique Chinese-ness—related to the influence of both the history and the present era.

Another illustrative case is the new gallery for the Anhui Museum. With Anhui being a crossroads of the north and south, we sought to convey the strength and honesty of northern China and the refinement and gentle nature of southern China to reflect both this cultural legacy and its inclusivity. In addition, the concepts of "inclusiveness" and a sense of "connection" needed to be present.

Reflecting the Zeitgeist

Architecture reflects the achievements of the socioeconomic sector, in addition to the achievements of science, technology, and culture. Our entry into a globalized information age has provoked profound changes in the realm of aesthetics and architectural values. The new concepts, new models, and new methods in design give architects access to a greater diversity of methods and trajectories.

Our practice in recent years can be characterized by the following features: "a reflection of the times";[4] the pursuit of a holistic, balanced layout (rather than symmetry) and a focus on flexibility; use of inverted triangle shapes to

create an antigravity effect; focus on visitor experience of space rather than linear, chronological narrative flow; and finally, attempts to respond to contemporary architectural vernacular by using topological geometry and complex architectural skins patterned with geometric shapes. It is worth noting that the goal of these new methods is to inspire visitors and lend a sense of cultural significance to the space.

In the design of Yantai Cultural Square, our team took advantage of the latest results developed across architecture and various other disciplines. The designer of the work deliberately emphasized asymmetry, continuity, and a sense of fluidity. We use an arrangement of folded plates and an irregular polyhedron form as a way to create an architectural signature. We adopted a strategy of aggregate space usage with a complex array of spaces. This enabled us to provide for a harmonious coexistence of multifunctional modules in a single site. With this strategy, we brought a visual realization of the essence of Yantai, a city known for its rolling fog and floating smoke, due to its seaside location and the construction of smoke signal towers in the 14th century.

Similarly, in our design for the Ningbobang Museum, which tells the story of a group of merchants in Ningbo, we employed the theme of collectivism, which is translated in a holistic way into the narrative structure of the space. We connected the central courtyard with water, and in linking these spaces express the cohesive nature of villages that were willing to defend and help each other.

Another element of our practice that speaks to this issue of zeitgeist is the use of contemporary materials as seen in the Qian Xuesen Library at Shanghai Jiaotong University and the Qinzhou Folk Culture Exhibition Center. For the library, our use of materials reflected contemporary aesthetic trends with a GRC-panel pixelated textured façade. The GRC panels were the finishing touch that created a sense of suspension and weightlessness, that endowed the architecture with a sense of strength and

Figure 23 Left: Yantai Cultural Center (2007). Right: Ningbo Group Museum.

power. For the Qinzhou Folk Culture Exhibition Center, we used a serrated stone curtain façade to evoke a fresh new look. The use of a serrated curtain allowed us to coordinate with and respond to the traditional construction materials, which in this case were gray bricks.

Conclusion

Looking back on more than 10 years of creating cultural architecture, we can summarize that on the one hand,

we have refined and developed the concept of the "Three Characteristics" (locality, culture, and a reflection of the times), while simultaneously in our designs, we paid great attention to the unique characteristics of each project. In particular, we developed a method for a probing and thorough research that enabled a decade-long exploration of cultural and "character-building" architecture.

All these efforts contributed to a path of innovation rooted in the characteristics of each locality.

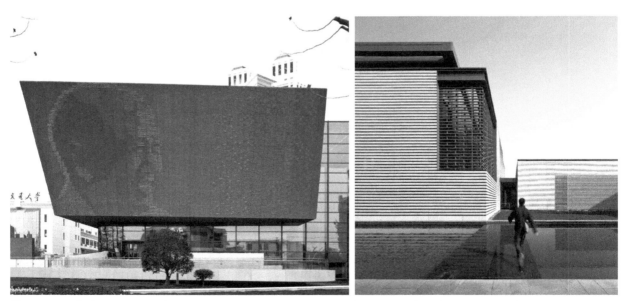

Figure 24 Left: Qian Xuesen Library in Shanghai Jiaotong University (2010) (part). Right: Qinzhou Folk Culture Exhibition Center (2011) detail.

11

CREATING BRIDGES BETWEEN CONTEMPORARY ART AND LIFE

Rebecca Catching

Working as a gallery director and museum curator in various Shanghai institutions for the past 16 years, I was frequently involved in showing visitors around—giving them the requisite hints to facilitate connections between individuals and works of contemporary art. In my various workplaces, I encountered all types of people, from the "neighborhood aunties" who were too shy to enter the gallery, to the *tuhao* nouveau riche collectors (chests all puffed up), to the hip *wenqing* or "cultured youth" filled with boundless curiosity. Despite the differences in age, education, and socioeconomic status, one common phrase was perpetually ringing through the galleries—"*kan bu dong*"—literally "seeing but not understanding." It was almost as if contemporary art was invented to baffle the willing visitor.

Viewer alienation from contemporary art is by no means confined to China. Though growing quickly, contemporary art museums in both China and the global West still attract fewer visitors than other kinds of museums.

One would think that, given the opportunity of initiating the public to new and innovative art forms, museums might make a greater effort in terms of education and interpretation, but unfortunately many are stuck in a top-down hierarchical "curator as king" model, with weak interpretive strategies.

Consider, for instance, this paragraph from the press release for the Yinchuan Biennale "Starting from the Desert: Ecologies on the Edge," held in 2018 at the Yinchuan Museum of Contemporary Art:

In search for eco-logics as a new paradigm of transversal thought, the Second Yinchuan Biennale attempts not to reduce these elements to subject matter, but to utilize them in order to question the limits of the exhibition format, and thus to eventually produce a new eco-model of exhibiting.

Such academic language is too often the norm in most contemporary art institutions in China and elsewhere. Despite the challenge of picking one's way through the dense thicket of verbiage, this particular biennale *actually* made a valiant attempt to reach out toward the local specificities of Yinchuan and its location on the edge of the Gobi Desert. This chapter will provide examples of how the Chinese contemporary art sector is developing strategies to help people relate to and understand contemporary art, often linking the art to a sense of place. "Starting from the Desert" explored topics such as ecology, minority culture, rural space, hybridization, and cultural exchange—all of these topics are inherently linked to the culture of Yinchuan as a desert city on the Silk Road. In addition, past exhibitions at Yinchuan MoCA have reinforced these local links, through the museum's collection of Qing dynasty oil paintings and antique maps. Though not very contemporary, they are well suited to the tastes of the demographic of the city, all the while dialoguing with Yinchuan as a place, a locus of intercultural exchange.

Guangzhou's Times Museum, designed by Rem Koolhaas to occupy the 14th floor of a residential compound, makes communicating with its community a key priority of its programming and scholarship. It has chosen the local urban village of Huangbian as an object of study for its Banyan Commune artist residency program. "Since we have

Figure 25 Visitors to the Shanghai Biennial at the Powerstation of Art (2012) experience the installation "Clockwise" by Spanish artist Cristina Lucas: a series of clocks in a 360-degree arc set at 4-minute intervals reflecting the global spread of modernity. *Photography: Rebecca Catching*

a rapidly changing landscape at Huangbian, and the relations we are building require a continuous dialogue as part of a long-term process," says Pan Siming, associate curator of the public programs department, "our medium-term strategy for the first five years involves selecting projects which are more dynamic and which promote strong social bonds with the communities."[1]

Pan and her colleagues spent hours walking the streets of Huangbian, reaching out to community leaders such as the Huangbian Neighborhood Committee, the manager of the Huangbian community WeChat social media channel, and various academics, artisans, and small business owners, to understand more about the people who are the heart of the neighborhood. In a recent project by Dutch artist Wapke Feenstra, the artist and curators engaged in extensive interactions with local leather workers. Huangbian is known as a leather manufacturing hub, and the artist interviewed various craftspeople in order to understand the history of the craft in the region, the scope of local skills and knowledge, and to make valuable personal connections. Feenstra produced a bag that was later sold in the museum gift shop, and the project was exhibited in the first-floor lobby space, which being on street level, receives a lot of walk-ins.

Beyond this kind of outreach, the museum has also courted a more specialized demographic through contributing to the independent art infrastructure of Guangzhou. The "Huangbian Station" project is both a platform for young artists (a shopfront where they can show their work) and also a kind of informal "school" where students must apply to join and partake in lectures from curators and artists. Huangbian Station was founded to provide an alternative to state-sponsored education by two former professors of the Guangzhou Academy of Fine Art, Huang Xiaopeng and Xu Tan, known for their work with the influential 5th Studio.[2] Thus, the museum seeks to reach out to different demographics, from leather workers to young art students, at the same time; projects on local issues become a bridge for the community residents who may not have a natural interest in contemporary art.

These kinds of local projects provide the dual benefits of raising the profile of the institution in the community and building an institutional understanding about the surrounding population.

Luxelakes A4 Museum, located in the upscale residential community in Tianfu New District in Chengdu, reaches out through local and participatory projects to not only the

Figure 26 At Luxelakes A4 Art Museum (2008, Chengdu), children participate in a site-specific public art project, "Wild Flower Field," at Antiquity Square, Chengdu IFS. *Photo courtesy: Luxelakes A4 Art Museum*

well-heeled residents of its gated community, but also to populations in the grittier parts of Chengdu.

It makes a concerted effort to cater to youngsters with a children's ecomuseum; open-ended, family-friendly exhibition guides (something rarely seen in China); and a children's art festival (iSTART) with animations, theater performances, and specially commissioned artworks, designed by artists to appeal specifically to a young audience.

But beyond this family focus, a lot of the art projects commissioned by the museum seek to understand the local cultural, political, and economic character of the city. For instance, "Secrets of the Streets: Chengdu," by the architecture research collective NOFFICE (Zhu Ye and Wei Hao), offered a tribute to local neighborhood culture (the kind *not* found in this posh community), presenting artifacts of community and street life including old pieces of furniture, big character posters, a *mah-jong* set, and announcements from the local neighborhood committees. This is a kind of "musealization" of these unglamorous but vital urban communities that, set in the context of Luxelakes, made a pointed critique. In addition to the Luxelakes location, "Secrets of the Streets: Chengdu" featured performances held in downtown neighborhoods. Another artist project by Chen Jianjun and Cao Minghao employed oral history to illuminate the communities that had previously inhabited Chengdu's river systems. "We gave the

artists the task of understanding the water systems of the whole geographic area of Chengdu," says exhibition and academic department director and curator Li Jie. "We learned that, historically, Chengdu used to be an inland Venice where the canals and the land routes were a very important means of transportation. The residents could open up the door of their house and step into a boat." In this context, says Li, artists become "workers of society," engaging with residents to collect rapidly disappearing oral histories. Seeking to transform this history into visual form, the artists worked with one of their informants, a woman named Mrs. Gong, teaching her basic painting skills. Mrs. Gong then produced a scroll painting depicting her recollections of life along the Chengdu waterways in the style of the famous painting "Along the River during the Qingming Festival."[3] The traditional style of painting had broad appeal, and the work was also shown in Mrs. Gong's home neighborhood; thus, the museum was able to extend its reach both beyond the gated walls of the Luxelakes community and the intimidating ramparts of contemporary art.

Also located within an upscale residential development, OCAT Xi'an makes a comprehensive effort to obtain support from both the city's network of museums and the city as a whole—trying to create a voice for the contemporary despite the heavy atmosphere of history that pervades the former capital. Says director Karen Smith, "We are committed to exploring relationships that might or might not exist specifically in Xi'an, between the art of the past and of now, using contemporary perspectives and practices."

Xi'an is, of course, a city known for a wealth of ancient objects, including the Terra Cotta Warriors and many storied institutions, yet despite being probably the most cosmopolitan city in northwest China, its populace is somewhat conservative compared to coastal cities. Smith's programming tries in earnest to plug into various facets of Xi'an's culture, making reference to its history in a way that is both intellectually challenging and enticing for the general public. For instance, Yao Qingmei's project "Sanzu Ding and Its Patterns" presents a riff on the construction of the past in the form of institutional critique. Smith describes it as a "fabulous faux archaeological research 'excavation.' . . . An entirely fabricated Neolithic community, complete with symbols and artifacts (pottery, axe heads, etc.) unearthed from a site near Xi'an." The artist framed this excavation with a series of documentaries—where she played the role of archaeologist, scholar, and workers—referencing the past and posing questions about the construction of history.

Another project, "Portrait of Xi'an," invites foreign artists to create a portrait of the city, thus using a familiar subject—a city much loved by its residents—as a starting point. An upcoming project with British artist Dryden Goodwin involved a collaboration with the local Cultural Relics Bureau, which had the added benefit of bridging the contemporary and the traditional, the state-run and the private, on both a personal and institutional level. Says Smith, "The project is to be overseen by the international office for world heritage sites in Xi'an, which will provide Dryden with full access to the contents and staff . . . all the ancient monuments, sites and museums in order to explore the people who work 'behind the scenes' to make, preserve, and promote history and heritage in China today."[4]

OCAT Xi'an also uses Xi'an's heritage as a jumping-off point for their educational programming in an effort to draw audiences who might be wary of long and often meandering academic talks. "With the aim of exploring the ties between the art of history and now, we do a lot of talks aimed at helping people engage with the topics. . . . History is not immutable. Ideas change with experience," says Smith. "We're not afraid to take it all apart and ask naïve questions. This helps break down barriers—the mind-sets of 'I don't understand' or 'it's got nothing to do with my life'—to looking, seeing, and learning to read art in ways that can be meaningful to each person."

Throughout these local contemporary art institutions—from Guangzhou, to Chengdu, to Xi'an—we can trace a common perspective to engage with their communities from a position of friendly curiosity and seek to make the acquaintance with their "nonvisitors"—the ones who have yet to pass through their doors. They create programming that suits the needs of *distinct* demographics, and while these institutions are respected for the rigor of their exhibition making and scholarship, they do not look down upon their viewers.

As with museum booms in the West (see chapter 4), there are failures too. Chengdu Museum of Contemporary Art recently had to scale back its activities.[5] The problems faced by Chinese private museums are, in fact, many, and frank discussion among the art community is bound to cause fidgeting and downcast glances. Within the supporting corporate entity, when the political winds blow, directors are forced to step down, no matter how well they are performing. This can often result in a kind of decapitation of the institution because the pyramidal management structure does not allow less-senior members of the staff to carry on as before.

Given the rudimentary state of philanthropy in China, private museums are also subject to the whims of their backers, who may decide to withdraw support. This is compounded by lack of planning experience, which leads to the bulk of the budget being spent on the initial construction costs with little set aside for operational costs, and even less spent on hiring and maintaining qualified personnel.

At the root of many failed museums we also find a "power-sharing" problem—the cultural conflict that often occurs between the financial backers and the museum staff. Financial backers are known to interfere on such matters as the selection of artists and even the minutiae of daily operations. They can be notoriously mercurial, stalling decisions or changing their minds at the last minute—the museum staff then scramble to adjust to the new strategy, wasting time and resources in the process.[6]

However, there are hopeful examples such as those in this chapter—Times Property Group, OCT Group, and Chengdu Wide Horizon Investment Group—where the property developers have demonstrated a true commitment to art, providing regular funding and supporting these institutions over the past decade (OCT for its part has four other museums in China). They also have allowed their teams significant freedom to innovate, remaining relatively "hands-off." In China, we see many examples of this kind of healthy model. Besides A4, Times Museum, and OCAT Xi'an there is the Rockbund Museum, Ullens Center for Contemporary Art, Redtory, Today Art Museum, and OCAT Shenzhen. Most are working with relatively modest budgets yet still manage to produce top-notch programming. These new museums demonstrate that, with the right attitude and devoted professional staff who are given the freedom to pursue interesting projects, the private contemporary art museum can both prove its relevance to the community and operate as a sustainable enterprise.

Rebecca Catching

PART III:
OPENING UP — TO THE WORLD

27 The Terra Cotta Warriors are some of China's most welcomed cultural ambassadors around the world.
Photography: hslo

12

CULTURAL DIPLOMACY AND SOFT POWER

An Laishun

Though China possesses a sophisticated culture of collecting over thousands of years, European-style museums did not take root in this country until the 20th century. They first began to emerge in China's cities along the eastern coast synchronized with west European missionaries, explorers, and scholars after the 1850s. For instance, the two earliest museums in China, the Ziccawei (or Heude Museum) and the Shanghai Museum, appeared in Shanghai in 1868 and 1874 respectively. Created by French missionary and zoologist Pierre Heude and explorer and amateur entomologist W. B. Pryer, the museums were located in Shanghai's French and International concessions. While Heude's museum was not very public facing, the Shanghai Museum, founded by the Royal Asiatic Society, eventually began to attract more Chinese visitors and adapted its collection to suit local tastes. Arthur de Carle Sowerby, one of the museum's directors, felt that the museum had a somewhat healing power, bringing people of all cultures together during a war-torn period in China's history.

> In a world that many people feel has gone mad with its terrible wars . . . international animosities and antagonisms, [museums] help humanity cling to its sanity by reason of their cultural appeal of all that is best in our civilization. In such institutions men and women of all nationalities meet in amity, forgetting the hostile arena of world politics, in pursuit of intellectual endeavors that know no racial boundaries.[1]

Though we may doubt Sowerby's overly optimistic words, the museum did eventually succeed in bringing different groups together and attracted a range of visitors according to Sowerby's observation (roughly one-third Westerners and two-thirds Chinese), with Hu Shih and Wu Lien-teh,

scholars who specialized in contemporary China and medicine respectively, being invited to join the museum board.[2]

Modern Chinese museums were born out of such historical encounters. Even the Nantong Museum, the first museum built by a Chinese citizen, Zhang Jian (1853–1926), was influenced by Japanese models such as the Osaka International Exhibition. In fact, the term *museum* in Chinese language (*Bo-Wu-Guan*, meaning a hall storing immense objects) was originally referred to as a *Bo-Lan-Guan*, a translation of a Japanese term. Nantong Museum had a close connection to Japan through its director Sun Yue, who had an avid interest in the country and spoke Japanese. The museum engaged in a very early international personnel exchange, inviting scholars from Korea, China, and Japan to help catalog its collection, checking the appropriate Latin names of plants and animals.[3]

These institutions, at first, faced some fierce resistance from the more conservative elements of society, namely the monarchy. The first generation of Chinese museum professionals had to walk a fine line between establishing this "imported" concept while at the same time negotiating with their audience, to adapt these forms to local purposes. The museum as an institution, however, did eventually receive support, for its power not only to modernize but to educate and unite; that their emergence occurred during a time when the country was not only deeply divided but also under attack, seems no coincidence.

Following the founding of the People's Republic of China in 1949, China turned to the socialist Soviet Union in search of a new museum system and imported the Soviet models. Museums at this time were seen as bases for

Figure 28 "Pathways to Modernism: American Art, 1865–1945," on show from September 2018 to January 2019 at the Shanghai Museum (1996), explored America's transition to a modern nation through the work of its artists. The exhibition was a collaboration between the Art Institute of Chicago and the Terra Foundation. *Photography: Rebecca Catching*

patriotic education with narratives focused on regional natural resources, ancient history, and the achievements of socialist construction.

Though China was quite closed until the end of the Cultural Revolution, there was nonetheless some contact with the outside world during this time. In 1946, China was invited to the first conference of International Council of Museums (ICOM), held at the Louvre, and though the Chinese delegate could not attend the event in person, China's symbolic presence would lead to the formation of the Chinese National Committee of ICOM in 1983. This represented a milestone, as it was one of the first international cultural non-governmental organizations (NGOs) that China participated in in the cultural sector with the support of the Chinese government.

Cultural diplomacy for China became a way to slowly nudge open the door, and exhibitions such as the 1973 touring show "Exhibition of Archaeological Finds of the People's Republic of China" traveled to 16 countries and regions in Europe, Oceania, Africa, and Asia, touring the world for five years. When the exhibition toured the National Gallery in Washington in 1975, it represented the largest-ever

exhibition held in the museum and was seen by almost 700,000 people—no doubt the crowd must have included a few Washington insiders. This project is considered to be the first successful attempt of people-to-people diplomacy. Since 1973, the exhibition exchanges have increased in volume and in quality, through both government-driven projects and privately initiated projects.

As relations between China and the West thawed in the 1980s, China saw another boom of museum building, and inside the exhibition halls, narratives began to change, moving away from issues of class struggle as museums began to incorporate theories and practices from a variety of countries, especially the ones from Europe and North America.

These practices were constantly being readjusted to suit China's political and cultural environment, and in the 1990s, after many years of relative isolation, China began slowly to engage in these kinds of exchanges. During the first decade of the 21st century, Chinese museums accelerated their internationalization process and evolved significantly in terms of their level of professionalism, integration of technology, and overall attitude toward the

An Laishun

visitor. Today Chinese museums are contributing actively to the conversation among world museums and providing valuable input and new potential models. Chinese museums are opening up to the world.

Thanks to the network provided by ICOM, the country has, over the past 36 years, been collaborating on both regional and international levels and establishing bilateral partnerships. In terms of the achievements of the Chinese National Committee of ICOM, China has promoted the ICOM Code of Ethics to become a well-known and accepted professional standard that helps govern the professionalism of Chinese museums as it does in many other countries.

The success of ICOM's 22nd General Conference in Shanghai, attracting some 3,500 museum delegates, showed the willingness of Chinese museums to become active members of the international community. In 2013, ICOM, ICOM China, and the Palace Museum jointly established the ICOM International Training Centre for Museum Studies—this constitutes the only ICOM training center in the world. For six years, the center has provided professional training and networking opportunities to 375 young museum professionals from 242 museums in 72 countries on all continents. Such interactions have helped provide a model for future collaborations, giving participants opportunities for cross-cultural dialogues and understanding.

In the past two decades, we've seen a tremendous increase in the number of outbound exhibitions and projects. Conservative estimates put the numbers at 840, counting not only those supported by the government but

private initiatives as well. Meanwhile, China is hosting many more international exhibitions, some of which have become wildly popular with the Chinese public. Two cultural events stood out in 2017: "A History of the World in 100 Objects," an exhibition from the British Museum (see chapter 19), held at the National Museum of China (Beijing) and Shanghai Museum, and "Age of Empires," held at the Metropolitan Museum of Art in New York and the National Museum of China, where crowds flocked to see exquisite jade funerary garments and rarely seen bare-chested strongmen from Emperor Qin Shihuang's tomb. The narrative of the exhibition explores how Qin and Han culture acted as dominant forces to merge various ethnic groups into one Chinese identity and ultimately a nation.

Another exceptional example of successful people-to-people diplomacy was the exhibition "China: Grandeur of the Dynasties," which opened in 2012 and toured to four cities in Japan between 2012 and 2013. This exhibition occurred during the most difficult period between the two countries since the normalization of Sino-Japanese diplomatic relations. Despite the political dispute between the two countries, cultural channels were kept open, and the exhibition was so well received that plans were immediately made to bring another exhibition, "China's Western Regions—Legends of the Silk Road," to Japan. Held from February 2013 to January 2014, it attracted some 139,000 Japanese visitors in Nagasaki alone. This kind of exchange proves that museums can play a big role in communication when words sometimes fail. Or to use the words of Arthur de Carle Sowerby, use the best our civilizations have to offer to help "humanity cling to its sanity."

13

EXHIBITIONS AS TOOLS OF DIPLOMACY

Zhou Ming

"As Richard Nixon's jet touched down at Beijing on the morning of February 21, 1972, a great transformation of Sino-American relations began. Two of the most populous yet politically and culturally different countries finally broke the isolation that they had created for each other over the past two decades."

This dramatic moment described by scholar Zhang Ru in his article "The Chinese Experience: Sino-American Arts Exchange"[1] represents a major milestone in the history of visual arts—as the Shanghai Communique expressed the will of both parties to engage in future cultural exchanges.

Nixon's visit was no doubt a milestone, but it by no means represents the *whole story*. Rather it might be useful to see it as a point on a continuum of exchange that predates the founding of America. The history of artistic exchange began much earlier and occurred between different global nodes of artistic production through both formal and informal channels.

Early History of Courtly Exchange, Jesuit Missionaries, Academic Exchange, and China's First Resident Artists

The first Western paintings were brought to China as early as 1601, by Matteo Ricci. Thomas H. C. Lee writes that in the Ming dynasty, there were a number of Renaissance and Baroque works circulating around China, brought by Jesuit priests, some of whom would actually take part in what we would now call an "artist in residency program." Missionaries such as Giuseppe Castiglione, who would stay for long periods, serving emperors Kangxi, Yong Zheng, and Qianlong at the Qing Court in the 18th century, acted as conduits for knowledge of Chinese and Western visual arts traditions. Castiglione, in fact, became a suc-

cessful painter; his portrait of Qianlong now hangs in the Yinchuan Museum. He was known for a unique fusion of Western and Chinese painting styles but also advised on the construction of palace architecture, for "Western-style palaces," such as the former Summer Palace. Again in the 18th century the Jesuits also played important roles in introducing Western painting techniques to China through the Tushanwan orphanage in Shanghai, where students learned Western techniques of oil painting and printmaking, taught in a systematic way. Though set up for practical purposes, to produce religious objects for the church, the school also helped lay the foundations for modern painting in Shanghai, as some of these students would later found their own art schools.[2]

For the first three decades of the 20th century, growing mobility and relative ease of travel led to many students going to France or Japan, studying in art academies and bringing back knowledge of Western art techniques and theory. Often Western ideas about art were filtered through Japan, and there was a great exchange of ideas and talent, with artists such as Uchiyama Kakichi working with author and artist Lu Xun to help reinvigorate and re-popularize the form of Chinese woodcuts.[3]

While this currency of ideas was flowing between China, Japan, and Western Europe, there was simultaneously an important form of exchange occurring between China and its closest neighbor, Russia/the USSR. Chinese early modern painting was highly influenced by mid-19th-century Russian painting, in particular a group of painters called The Wanderers, a group of realist painters whose subjects included landscapes and scenes of everyday life. They tended to focus on folk culture, but also on social injustice. Their impact can be seen in the popularization of Realism (and later Socialist Realism), which was once considered suspect by the Chinese artistic establishment. Many top Chinese artists were sent to study at the Repin Academy, and Wanderer Konstantin Maximov was officially invited by the Chinese government in 1954 for a three-year residency to instruct Chinese artists in realist technique and the composition and creation of history paintings.

Outbound Travel: Chinese Exhibitions Abroad from 1950 to 1980

Though the sort of "person-to-person" exchange outlined above would wane during the three decades following Liberation and the founding of the People's Republic of China in 1949, there nonetheless remained some exchange, mostly in the form of traveling exhibitions.

Even then, in the early days of the PRC, it was obvious that cultural objects were valuable props in the drama of diplomacy, with Premier Zhou Enlai bringing a selection of 12 artifacts from the Palace Museum in Beijing and exhibiting them in the Chinese delegation conference room in a sort of "show-and-tell" at the Geneva Convention. These symbols of a storied history no doubt lent credence to what was at the time a newly formed government. (For more on this topic of cultural artifacts and power see chapter 6.)

Figure 29 "Treasures of Chinese Art" at the Petit Palais (City of Paris Museum of Fine Arts) in May 1973. The exhibition was the most comprehensive exhibition of Chinese art abroad since 1935, when the "International Exhibition of Chinese Art" in London helped generate international support for China during the Japanese occupation of Manchuria. *Photo courtesy: Zhou Ming*

The first formal exhibition exchange after 1949 was held with the Soviet Union; "Chinese Art Exhibition" included over 600 artifacts and artworks from the neolithic period to the Ming and Qing dynasties. The exhibition held over four months attracted over 300,000 curious Russians, eager to see artifacts from a close yet culturally dissimilar neighbor. This would mark the beginning of a period of exchange with other ideologically friendly nations such as the Czech Republic and Romania.

In the 1960s, we saw the scope of artifact exchange expand with the "Yongle Palace Chinese Mural Exhibition," "Chinese Ancient Porcelain Exhibition," and "Xi'an Tablet Rubbings Exhibition," which toured in Tokyo and other cities in Japan. Warmly welcomed by the Japanese citizens, these two exhibitions received 350,000 and 200,000 visitors respectively. The exhibitions marked the beginning of cultural exchanges from the province of Shaanxi, a major powerhouse of ancient culture in terms of the number and quality of artifacts, most notably the ever-popular Terra Cotta Warriors.

The next major exhibition of antiquities happened in the 1970s, when "Unearthed Cultural Relics from the People's Republic of China" toured in 16 countries and regions including Europe, Oceania, Africa, and Asia from 1973 to 1978. More than 600 relics were seen by over six million visitors. In terms of the length of time touring and number of destinations, this was the most ambitious touring exhibition staged by China in the last century, and it amounted to an important diplomatic exercise at a time when China limited contact with other nations.

In the 1970s, as a détente was reached with many Western nations, there was an increase in the volume of exhibitions, with 30 touring shows sent to 17 countries around the world and a total viewership of 9 million. The 1980s saw that number rise to 50 exhibitions in 21 countries and 20 million viewers, and though the 1990s saw a brief dip in the intensity of cultural exchange (40 exhibitions and 13 million viewers), the last two decades have seen exhibition exchanges rising in tandem with China's economic prosperity. This increase is due, in no small part, to the efforts of NCHA (National Cultural Heritage Administration),[4] which helped facilitate a total of 840 exhibitions—six times the total number of previous years.

Along with NCHA, a number of other actors were quite important in facilitating these exchanges, such as Art Exhibitions China, the Shaanxi Cultural Exchange Center, the Palace Museum, the National Museum of China, and the Shanghai Museum. Through these exchange exhibitions, many cultural institutions in China have established long-term relationships with museums around the world.

During this time, there was something of a "trade surplus" in museum exchange, with exhibitions of antiquities traveling outbound but relatively few traveling inbound. Notable of these domestically hosted exhibitions was a painting exhibition by the Boston Museum of Fine Arts in 1979, which for many Chinese artists and art enthusiasts provided a first glance at abstract painting. The exhibition was not without controversy, given that abstraction was then seen as a radical "bourgeois form," but it would have great influence on the art of future generations.

Art as a Diplomatic Tool

The 1980s and Reform and Opening-Up were marked by the increasingly fluid travel of both people and objects. Zhang writes that following the normalizations of relations with the United States, the country saw a flood of diplomatic delegations, as many as 100 Chinese delegations a month. "Furthermore, the use of arts exchange to consolidate the general relationship, and to win US economic technological cooperation made arts exchange the handmaiden of diplomacy."[5] Arts events, he writes, take on a very symbolic nature in terms of diplomacy, and in bilateral relations, "the art itself was often secondary."[6] Arts exchanges were used by both sides for diplomatic purposes, but also by the Americans and some other Western countries to promote their own values and by the Chinese to gain international prestige.

On July 14, 1995, then-President Jiang Zemin and his delegation visited an exhibition of Chinese art during Jiang's visit to Germany. Jiang and German president Roman Herzog both traveled to view "Man and God in Ancient China," and a few years later in 1999, "The Golden Age of Chinese Archeology: Celebrated Discoveries from the People's Republic of China" toured the National Gallery in Washington, the Museum of Fine Arts in Houston, and the Asian Art Museum in San Francisco. As a sign of friendship and commitment to cultural exchange, the preface of the exhibition was purportedly written by President Jiang Zemin and President Clinton.

While at the time many Americans thought of China as a struggling nation just emerging from behind the bamboo curtain, this exhibition reminded them that China possessed a sophisticated civilization centuries before America had even hoisted up the star-spangled banner. Writing of this exhibition in the *Washington Post*, Paul Richard reported breathlessly:

> Gold gleams in the shadows, and snakes as swift as flames swarm over its bronzes, and bold, shape-shifting spirits, whose eyes are always on us, whose names we do not know, stare out of its ivories, its turquoises and jades, and nothing here is trivial, and everything is old. In car-honking

America, where early Beanie Babies are valued as antiques, these objects carry with them the silent, dreadful weight of vastness of time.

Again using the Nixon visit as a milestone, he goes on to explain that, at the time of the visit, two-thirds of these objects had yet to be discovered[7]—still buried in the fields of Chinese peasants.

The warming of diplomatic relationships continued in January 2004, during President Hu Jintao's special visit to Paris to commemorate the 40th anniversary of the establishment of diplomatic relations between China and France. In celebration of the Year of France in China, the Champs-Élysées was closed off for a parade that included dancing dragons and over 300 cultural events around Paris.[8] While there, the two leaders visited a Confucius exhibition in Musée Guimet in Paris, accompanied by French President Jacques Chirac. Ten years later, Musée Guimet hosted another exhibition in celebration of the 50th anniversary of diplomatic relations, "Splendeurs Des Han: Essor de l'Empires Celeste," the event inaugurated by Chinese president Xi Jinping and French president François Hollande.

Reflecting the history of China's diplomatic exchanges, "China: Three Rulers 1662-1795" went on show at London's Royal Academy in 2005. Hu Jintao and Queen Elizabeth cut ribbons to celebrate these imperial collections of three emperors: Kang Xi, Yong Zheng, and Qian Long, the same emperors that Italian painter Castiglione had served under. The works, on loan from the Palace Museum, told stories of the connections between art and power and the exchanges between China and the West during the 16th and 17th centuries. At the time, Hu Jintao even spoke on the influence of these antiquities exhibitions in diplomacy, commenting that antiquities are able to play roles that diplomats are unable to play.

No doubt one of China's most welcomed cultural ambassadors are the Terra Cotta Warriors, first displayed at the British Museum in September 2007. In order to properly welcome them, the British Museum invested two million dollars in customizing a spectacular temporary exhibition hall in the circular reading room. "The First Emperor: China's Terracotta Army" was the largest exhibition of Terra Cotta Warriors since the opening of the British Museum, and the objects themselves were supplemented with further interpretation in the form of videos, photographs, and texts to create a comprehensive experience. The exhibition received a constant influx of visitors on a daily basis, with total numbers approaching 850,000—which made it one of the most popular exhibitions in the history of the British Museum. Members of the British royal family, former British prime minister Gordon Brown, and British government leaders all paid tribute to the warriors. The exhibition cata-

logs sold well for many years even after the exhibition and have seen several reprints, including distribution in major European and American museums and bookstores.

In 1998, the charm offensive turned toward America, with "China 5,000 Years: Innovation and Transformation in the Arts" on show at the Guggenheim from February to June 1998, seeing 450,000 viewers over five months. Holland Cotter, writing in the *New York Times*, praised the collection of objects and spoke highly of a section curated by scholars Julia F. Andrews and Kuiyi Shen, which covered the era from 1850 to 1980, exploring the changes in ink painting with the introduction of Western influences and the era of Soviet-influenced Chinese Socialist Realism.[9]

More recently, China has expanded its cultural engagement beyond these traditional East-West routes, making connections with Japan, Latin America, and the Middle East. On November 21, 2016, President Xi Jinping and Peruvian president Pedro Pablo Kuczynski Godard made symbolic appearances at the "China-Latin Cultural Exchange Year" held in Lima, Peru, and visited the exhibition "Global Neighborhood—A Journey of China's Treasures in Peru."

We can see that these kinds of exhibitions can be crucial in bolstering national cultural agendas such as the One Belt, One Road initiative launched in 2013, which aims to improve "regional connectivity" and to place China in a more pivotal role in international affairs (for more on OBOR see chapter 5 of this book). In that context, "The Roads of Arabia—Archaeological Treasures of Saudi Arabia" exhibition was on show at the National Museum of China from December 2016 to March 2017 and featured almost 500 pieces gathered from various museums in Saudi Arabia. The extensive exhibition provided insight into the evolution of the archaeological culture of Saudi Arabia throughout the Stone Age, the prehistoric period, the pre-Islamic period, the Islamic period, and the birth of the modern Saudi Kingdom. These precious objects unearthed along the Spice Route and the various pilgrimage routes spoke of the exchanges and interactions between Arab culture and other Eastern and Western cultures inside and outside the Arabian Peninsula. This highly publicized exhibition was shown in China in support of a strategic partnership between China and Saudi Arabia.

The exhibition served the function of placing China within the greater context of the countries that surround it. The human-shaped stone tablets on show in the exhibition quickly became popular emojis among Chinese netizens; posted and reposted, their adorable expressions became ubiquitous. "In fact, given our distance from the Middle East, we are not very familiar with the desert and its civilization," one viewer remarked. "Many relics have an inextricable connection with China, from which Chinese elements can be identified. As such, we find that cultures are interconnected."

Cultural initiatives tend to follow political rapprochements, and it is common in China for projects in both the public and private spheres to be caught off-guard by the sudden political events that put their projects at risk. At the same time, these cultural exchanges can go some ways to maintaining a base level of connection and civility between nations, especially when relationships are tense.

At the beginning of the 21st century, the Sino-Japanese relationship was at a low ebb. Therefore, a series of art exhibitions were organized in Japan by NCHA. In 2004, the discovery of the epitaph of Sei Shinsei—a *kentoshi* or Japanese emissary dispatched to China during the Tang dynasty—provided the perfect occasion for an exchange. Acting as a reminder of the two countries' shared history, this find caused a great sensation in both China and Japan,

attracting hundreds of thousands of visitors. Many scholars wrote articles about the discovery, advocating the idea of using history as a mirror for the future. In August 2005, when "The Kentoshi and Art in the Tang Dynasty" was displayed at the Tokyo National Museum, the Japanese emperor and empress visited this exhibition, along with the president of the Japan-China Friendship Association, Hirayama Ikou, who delivered an address during the opening ceremony. "Today, in the 21st century, there have been some ups and downs in the relations between Japan and China, which have caused many people to worry," he said. "But the discovery of Kentoshi's epitaph made me feel as if I was hearing a cry from over 1,200 years ago, which called for the Japanese and Chinese people to live together in harmony." The power of this exhibition lay not only in its ability to bring two cultures together for a common experience but also to see ourselves in a continuum of history, rather than focus on a particularly painful recent instance of disagreement.

14

NAVIGATING CROSS-CULTURAL COLLABORATIONS—A CURATORIAL PERSPECTIVE

Chen Shen

The speed and development of museums over the last three or four decades in China still continues to boggle the mind. Young people under the age of 25 could hardly even recognize what the museums of cities such as Wuhan looked like in the mid-1980s. But I remember, as I was born in Hubei, a native of Wuhan and a student of archaeology at Wuhan University, located near the Hubei Provincial Museum.

A Short Memoir

Now known as one of the top 15 museums in China, in the 1980s, its Soviet Union–style, match-box-type building displayed a series of world-renowned artifacts including some magnificent bronze bells. They were in fact from the largest set of suspended bronze bells in China, dating to the third century BCE. These bells were part of an instrument called a *bianzhong*, a set of bells on racks big enough to occupy a small room. In 1978 they were unearthed during an excavation of the Marquis Yi, in Zeng State. I remember how the gallery of Hubei ancient history, which focused on the rebellion uprising and farmer revolution of the so-called federalist dynasties, was illuminated by fluorescent lamps, at least one of which was always out of order and buzzing continuously as the light struggled to flicker on. Artifacts, which seemed to be valuable only to archaeologists and historians, were displayed within a long case along the walls of the rectangular gallery, and objects were placed with a business card–size label of black ink on white paper noting the object name, date, and location where it was unearthed. The museum building was empty most of the time, except when school visits were scheduled during the spring session. But there were always two or three ladies sitting on a bench behind a wooden classroom table at the end of the gallery, either gossiping about their neighbors or office mates or quietly knitting, their attention locked on to the movements of their needles. Attempts to get their attention were mostly futile. These gallery sitters probably didn't know, or care to know, that most of these notable objects on display were replicas—a fact that was not mentioned on the labels, or shared in any way with the public.

Of course, this museum experience is now gone, swept away by the winds of the Reform and Opening-Up, along with the original building. A new building stands in its place and in fact more than that, a new landscape. The real set of bells and associated artifacts dug out from the tomb, the gold objects, bronze vessels, lacquers, and jades from the tomb of the famous icon of the Warring States were seen together for the first time in Tokyo, Japan, in 1992, even before the residents of Wuhan were able to view them. But today, the complete set of the Zeng Houyi bells are considered national treasures, forbidden to travel to foreign lands and now permanently suspended in a brand-new museum gallery where they are viewed by millions of visitors every year.

In the early summer of 2004, I sat among more than a dozen departmental heads and managers of the museum, following lectures with the museum staff. Invited by Wang Hongxing, the former director of Hubei Provincial Museum, I was asked to speak with his team about museum operations in Western museums, including collection management, registration, conservation, exhibition planning and design, as well as education and learning. I scratched my head and drained my brain of the cumulative knowledge of eight years of working experience at the Royal Ontario Museum (ROM) in Toronto. Wang was the chief archaeologist at the provincial institute of archaeology and had graduated from the same department as I, only four years earlier. We shared the same passion for archaeology, and were both working in museums. However, Wang did not have any prior museum experience before he took the position as director. Wang had a vision at the time, as he told me in person: "museums are made for visitors, not for researchers like archaeological institutes." A few months later, he and one of his associates visited the ROM. During a tour of the galleries, I introduced one of our senior volunteers to him. Next thing I knew he and my friend, who had worked at ROM as a volunteer for over 40 years, sat on a gallery bench conversing for over an hour and a half. It was Wang's first exposure to a brand-new concept largely unheard of in Chinese museums, but seemingly very common in Western museums. That concept was volunteering, and he seized upon it with gusto.

For the next few years, Wang fashioned his museum to be a model for the transformation and modernization of museums (especially at the provincial level). Many practices of Chinese museum management, like their Western counterparts, were implemented in this early stage during the turn of the century. By 2007, the Hubei museum had transformed itself from a dark, quiet, sterile setting, into a crowded, park-like, dynamic environment.

In my view, Wang's beliefs about "museums being made for the public" have had the most significant impact on Chinese museum development in the first decade of the 21st century. Certainly the general principles of New Museology are not unique to Hubei, but I think it's worth pointing out that the free-admission system now adopted by Chinese state-run museums, a practice that began in 2008, started in Hubei Provincial Museum as a trial run one year earlier under Wang's leadership. The free-admission policy in China has totally transformed how these mu-

Figure 30 "The Warrior Emperor and China's Terracotta Army" exhibition, Garfield Weston Exhibition Hall, July 2010, at the Royal Ontario Museum. *Photography: Brian Boyle, MPA, FPPO. Photo courtesy: The Royal Ontario Museum © ROM.*

Chen Shen

seums operate. They have departed significantly from their former stern and conventional presence now that millions of viewers are streaming through their doors.

Chengdu: Building the New Audiences

The same transformation in state-run provincial museums can also be witnessed at the Sichuan Provincial Museum. In 2002, when my colleagues Tricia Walker, a ROM registrar, and Cathy Stewart, a ROM conservator, traveled there to carry out a condition report on a returned loan of a major exhibition, "Treasures from a Lost Civilization: Ancient Art from Sichuan," they watched uneasily as the Sichuan Museum staff hand-carried the objects through a dark and dusty corridor up and down the stairs. There was nothing they could do about it! However, this practice is a thing of the past, and something that won't be encountered by my colleagues who go to Chinese museums today. As a matter of fact, they are now shocked by the state-of-the-art hardware found in all new Chinese museums. In 2017, while accompanying an exhibition loan from the ROM's Egyptian collection to the Jinsha Archaeological Museum in Chengdu (see below), my colleague was pleasantly surprised by the professionalism and passion of the museum staff. They installed a beautiful exhibition showcasing objects, most of which had been, until then, hidden away in the ROM's storage rooms. Thanks to the Jinsha Museum, these objects were able to have a new life in China and were viewed by almost 600,000 visitors in a period of four months.

Before I return to the ROM's Egyptian exhibition in China, I would like to stress the incredible pace at which this development is occurring. When I organized an exhibition with loans from the Sanxingdui archaeological site, I visited Chengdu many times between 2001 and 2002. During one trip, I visited a new archaeological site, which was later identified as one of the most important discoveries of the new century—the Jinsha site. The discovery suggested that descendants of the mysterious Sanxiangdui people migrated to Chengdu 3,000 years ago, from a place called Guanghan, roughly 100 kilometers outside the city. When I stood on the edge of the excavation units, I took photos of remains such as carnivore teeth or stone bi discs, noticing that the site was in the middle of a real estate housing project. Fifteen years later, the landscape covering the site had become part of a park that was enjoyed by local residents. The gold, jade, and other treasures are now showcased in the gallery and have become part of the museum. The carnivores' teeth that I took photos of were still there on the ground as part of an on-site display. When I returned in 2018 on a tour with 20 ROM members, Ms. Wang Fang, deputy director of the Jinsha Museum, told me the museum welcomed nearly 1.2 million visitors in 2017 when they celebrated their 10th anniversary. At the time,

I had just received news that the ROM had 1.44 million paid visitors during the same year, the highest number in the history of the museum, but this is of course after being open in Toronto for 104 years.

But if we think that Jinsha's visitor numbers are record-breaking, then we need to think again. Chengdu Museum is a municipal museum of art on the city's most popular and iconic Tianfu Square. Sitting in a café on the top of a six-story modern building overlooking the square, we can see a 30-foot-tall statue of Chairman Mao waving his right hand, surrounded by colorful banners and flowers. This view is probably one of the biggest "must-sees" for tourists. Within five years and 1.2 billion RMB in construction costs later, the Chengdu Museum opened its doors to the public in 2016, welcoming 1.54 million visitors in the first year, of course with free admission. In 2017, visits increased to 2.6 million, a 58 percent increase within one year. When I asked how the museum was able to accomplish this, the museum's director of marketing and communications, Ms. Xiao Feige, said: through special exhibitions with popular appeal and down-to-earth public programming. The stand-out gallery of Chengdu Museum has to be the shadow puppet collection. Despite being at the end of a long and tiring day of sight-seeing, ROM members found this gallery to be the highlight of the day. Xiao got her professional training in France with a master's degree in art history; she also served as a curator for the special touring exhibition "Paths of Modernity—French Modern and Contemporary Painting." The exhibition ran 79 days and received 530,000 visitors.

It is clear that the Chengdu Museum is not a one-off success story, as we see such strong attendance figures repeated in new museums, and new branches of old museums, all across the nation. The museum doors are open to millions of visitors who never imagined 30 years ago that museums could be *such* attractive tourist destinations. Xiao touches on an important point, that Chinese museums are now seeking more and more opportunities to bring in interesting international traveling exhibitions, in order to meet the demands and expectations of their new audiences. Not long ago, in 2004, I was invited by the National Cultural Heritage Administration (NCHA) and Sichuan University to a special workshop. The two-week workshop was designed under the state administration request for a training for Chinese museum directors. This is where I met then Hubei Provincial Museum Director Wang Hongxing for the first time, although we had heard of each other through our colleagues. The topic I was assigned to was the management and practice of traveling exhibitions in Western museums. At that time, Chinese museums were only interested in sending out their exhibition packages to Western museums, as a means of training staff in museum practices and building their understanding of how things work. What I emphasized in my talk was how to create relevant content for exhibition proposals, rather than the usual focus on the quality and magnificence of local or regional treasures. I alluded to how the ROM must assess the costs of borrowing based on information submitted by the museum. At the time I felt my lectures were just words floating on the breeze, but a decade later, my colleagues and I find ourselves in the middle of negotiations to borrow collections from the ROM with a number of Chinese museums. The message is clear: new audiences want to see more non-Chinese culture and heritage from other Western museums—museums they are becoming acquainted with on their vacations abroad. They want to see more artworks from the collections of world-renowned museums like the British Museum, the Metropolitan Museum of Art, and the ROM.

Cross-Cultural Exhibitions

The ROM is Canada's largest museum of art, culture, and nature, and we have had the great fortune to work with cultural institutions from China for many decades. The ROM had the privilege to host an inaugural exhibition of art and archaeology from China in 1974 before the tour continued to Washington, D.C., and San Francisco, when China and U.S. relations were beginning to defrost. During my own tenure at the ROM, I organized three major exhibitions from China, and thus witnessed the incredible changes and developments of Chinese museums and cultural institutions, which have had an immense influence in today's relationship between Chinese and Western museums.

Nanjing Museum was founded as the Central Museum of the Republic of China in 1933, and became a leading museum in Jiangsu Province after 1949. The Nanjing Museum and Royal Ontario Museum have had a partnership since 2008, as part of a cultural exchange of sister provinces (Jiangsu and Ontario). Both museums are provincial agencies, and both are on a high level of national prominence in terms of collections and research.

Both museums have worked together to fulfill collaborative commitments by producing a joint exhibition titled "Pharaohs and Kings: Treasures from Ancient Egypt and China's Han Dynasty." Instead of a conventional one-way loan exhibition, the exhibition showcased 155 objects from the ROM's Egyptian collection alongside 200-plus objects from the Han dynasty collection of the Nanjing Museum, giving visitors a unique experience of cross-cultural comparison and helping them understand the natural and the supernatural, the life and the afterlife of two different civilizations. The exhibition won the award of top 10 exhibitions in the year 2016. But behind the success, there were some challenges faced by both parties.

The first challenge we encountered was "timing and scheduling." Timing is everything, and somehow some things had to happen at the wrong time for a right reason. Our Chinese colleagues are accustomed to working on very tight but workable schedules, while our Western colleagues are used to working within standard Western timelines. At the ROM, a normal loan process takes about 10 to 12 months, but for an exhibition of 155 objects, including human and animal mummies, we required additional time for conservation treatment, which meant that we needed a much longer time frame than the standard year. At the beginning, both museums had planned for at least a one-year lead time, but a situation led to some very special circumstances occurring at the beginning of the year that required this special exhibition to open six months earlier than planned. ROM staff had to prepare everything, including conservation treatments, curatorial labels, insurance evaluation, mounting, packing, and shipping within six months. We understood the significance and implications of this project, set our priorities with support from museum senior management, and carefully allocated and coordinated resources and the schedules of various departments, building in effective communications and efficient workflow to save time. But of course all of this could not be accomplished without incurring costs, which both museums agreed would be built into the overall exhibition budget. I appreciated the Nanjing Museum's acknowledgment of this necessity, and the diligence of ROM staff that was the key to solving the issues of timing in this project.

The next challenge was conservation. ROM conservators might have rejected the loan of several metal objects based on the Nanjing Museum's facility report. The Nanjing Museum had set its microclimate control for metal objects at a relative humidity level of 45 to 50 percent, which we later understood was China's national standard. ROM's practice, which is similar to many North American museums, set RH levels at 20 to 25 percent for metals, especially for archaeological metals. So ROM conservators and designers spent a great deal of time and effort to provide design sketches and even built a special case to indicate the required amounts of silica gel to reduce the RH levels. In addition, the Nanjing Museum's conservation team created an innovative electronic microclimate control device that met our requirements. The unit was successfully tested one month prior to the opening. The problem was resolved through an innovative conservation tool that could be used in future exchange exhibitions.

The safety of the artifacts is always a primary concern for traveling exhibitions, and part of this process involves transportation. Selecting the right shipping carrier is a serious matter for the lender. Like many museums who have worked with China, the ROM has had great experiences in previous exhibitions with one of China's best fine art shipping companies, Huaxie. We intended to make detailed requests for a specific shipping company for the best interests of our museum, but we also needed to respect Nanjing Museum's normal tendering procedures for selection. While differences of opinions occurred, transparent and honest communication was vital to establishing the best interests of both museums. As we have experienced, there are always last-minute surprises that occur during travel and at customs, which can affect the installation schedule. It is sensible that both museums agree upon a company that has ample experience working with government agencies and understands international practices.

The last challenge I would like to mention here is the "communication" between representatives of two parties. The communication challenge is in fact embedded in all the other challenges and problems mentioned above. We understand that the organization of Chinese museums places them under various subgroups within the museum, such as the cultural exchange department, foreign affairs department, or the administrative department, which might have staff with bilingual capability or who understand different cultural backgrounds. However, we can often encounter hurdles when talking about specialized topics such as conservation, registration, object mounting, and installation. All of these specialized topics need to be negotiated through one person, the main contact, who has to transfer the original inquiries to the project team members. Sometimes technical terminology is lost in translation during the communications, which results in circular conversations that stall the resolution of the issue. This project was no exception, but at least both museums were quick to recognize the need for direct conversations between the conservators of the two museums. In particular, we were fortunate to have a Nanjing Museum conservator assigned to the project, who was trained in the West with perfect English. She was able to communicate directly with ROM conservators, which resulted in accurate understanding and was extremely time efficient.

Communication, Communication, Communication

I would like to conclude that the key to a successful collaboration like this is communication, communication, and communication. In fact, I will use three different Chinese phrases that, in their respective contexts, would be translated into the same English word. First is to communicate in direct dialogues *duihua* 对话 between project team members on specific aspects of responsibilities. We do need centralized support and a consistent voice in negotiations, but operationally we encourage Chinese team members like registrars, conservators, art handlers, and curators to be more present in direct dialogue with Western museum teams when detailed requirements are put forward. I refer to the second communication, which is to be transparent and honest about conversations *jiaoliu* 交流 that are built on good faith in the hopes of making the collaboration work. Both sides can benefit greatly from open discussions about the needs and priorities of each museum, and such discussions should lead to adjustments of approaches and to corresponding changes in work plans. The third aspect of communication is to broaden mutual understanding *lijie* 理解 between the East and the West. Communication is needed to understand our cultural differences, differences in work procedures, and differences in work ethics. These differences also need to be addressed internally within each institution; for example, the ROM's conservators were finally able to understand that Chinese museums have quite a different conservation mandate and work standard on exhibitions. In the end, each team adjusted their provisions and requirements in a way that worked better for both museums. This led to a successful project—our Egyptian exhibition at Nanjing Museum—which not only resulted in a popular show but built up a greater *lijie* or understanding of how museums function on the other side of the globe.

15

CHANGING CONCEPTS AND STRATEGIES FOR PUBLIC ENGAGEMENT

Tomislav Sola

China's fifty centuries of civilization and twenty-two of continuous statehood constitute an inexhaustible and practically unfathomable collective experience. In the West, the public museum experience correlates strongly with the development of the nation-state and the consequent need to translate scholarly, monarchical, and religious collections to the modern purposes of national identity, industrialization, and colonization. The rapid expansion of public museums in China correlates to their modern history as described elsewhere in this book,[1] but does, of course, run in parallel to some of the currents that characterized the development of museums in the West. This chapter, by a close Western observer, written through the lens of heritage development, seeks to address the changing strategies of public engagement during China's museum building boom.

Transitioning from Centralized Control to Collaborative Exhibition Making

Shaanxi Museum is located in the ancient city of Xi'an—famous for the nearby archaeological site where the Terra Cotta Warriors were buried. It is firstly one of the oldest museums in China (1919)[2] and also one of the largest after its modernization in 1983–2003. Along with museums in Shanghai, it innovated a relatively open mode of governance by including community leaders and experts on the museum's advisory board to guide and direct the development programs and the strategic management of the museum. The lack of human resources, on the other hand, forced the museum to turn to local universities, research institutes, and other providers of services. Using

this unconventional model, the museum was not only outsourcing many routine jobs, but entrusting research to external experts in exchange for the equivalent of staff remuneration. In this model, the leadership retains control of the quality of the work produced by these "contracted researchers." These exhibitions combined research, science, and entertainment to create elaborate participatory exhibitions that were seen by more than one million visitors per year. "Our curators introduced new studies to the public through these sensitive exhibitions, which brought unfamiliar archaeological finds and rigorous science much closer to public life."[3]

Part of engaging with the public is not just engaging with the visitors but also enabling deeper interactions through docent and volunteer programs. China's tradition of volunteerism dates back to the times of Confucius, who advocated kindness and benevolence not only to one's family but also to the state. This was echoed by other Chinese philosophical traditions and augmented by Western philanthropic notions that came to China in the mid-19th century. Volunteerism began to seriously catch hold after 1949 through the figure of Lei Feng[4]—an actual soldier whose service was somewhat mythologized into a string of outrageous acts of sacrifice for his fellow army men. The "spirit of Lei Feng" is synonymous with selflessness and service to the public good and lives on in many local volunteer organizations. Much of volunteering in China is tied to the government, which has the resources to mobilize huge numbers of volunteers for events such as the Beijing Olympics (70,000 volunteers) and the Shanghai Expo. Yet despite this rich tradition, up until recently, many museums did not have well-developed programs to recruit and train volunteers.

Suzhou Museum took the lead in demonstrating that a friendly atmosphere in a museum can provide the perfect setting for the museum experience for contemporary audiences.[5] When the museum was deemed "Best Creative Museum in China" by the Chinese Museums Association (CMA) in 2013, it was mainly for its pioneering role in developing volunteer services. Their organizational structure, their training, recruitment methods, clearly structured responsibilities, and level of engagement that reached well outside the museum's walls made the museum a model in China. In addition, volunteerism that creates the atmosphere of citizens working for citizens acts as an embodiment of a traditional socialist ideal (for more on Suzhou Museum's volunteer program see chapter 22).

Using Information Technology to Streamline Operations and Improve Outreach

Though many museums have keenly embraced new forms of technology such as Quick Response (QR) codes, we are beginning to see a broader adoption of digital technologies

not only in the sense of digitizing collections but also in the sense of using data to understand more about visitor experience. Museums received a big push to improve their integration of technology in 2016 when Xi Jinping put forth his "Internet+" strategy, which encourages traditional industries to incorporate information technology (for instance, cloud computing or big data) into their operations in order to create a more innovative environment for development. This came under the umbrella of the policy Internet Power, known as *Wangluo Qiangguo*, which declared China's ambitions to become an Internet superpower.[6] This proclamation created ripples in the museum world and a drive toward digital outreach and boundary-free museums.

Dr. Wei Jun, director of the Guangdong Museum, proclaimed that under the guidance of the No-Boundary Museum concept, "[Museums] should break through the limitations of their physical space, and actively expand exhibitions, activities, and resources into public spaces such as cities and communities in a physical or digital sphere."

This might not at first seem revolutionary, but given that 10 to 15 years ago Chinese museums often struggled to keep their websites regularly updated, this leap into the public

Figure 31 Visitors explore the collection of the Shanghai Museum (1996) through an interactive screen. Selected images feature information and descriptions of the museum's collection. *Photography: Rebecca Catching*

Tomislav Sola

realm represented a bold step. The adoption of digital technologies naturally helped the museum reach its public in a relatively simple and efficient manner, but these technologies were also implemented in order to streamline operations. These "smart museums" sought to employ data to facilitate everything from scheduling to the construction of exhibits.[7] From conservation information management to micro and macro environmental monitoring, to smart services, to multimedia digital interactives—the Guangdong Museum has expanded its physical and virtual space in an attempt to break down the boundaries between the museum and its users.

What is interesting in this case study is that technology is taken less as mere technique and more as a new "mindset"; there is a new freedom of innovation that seems to result in plenty of public-friendly innovations. This seems to be happening fairly rapidly in Chinese museums. The Palace Museum in Beijing is immense, and it is an institution that is symbolically central to Chinese identity; so when innovation happens at the Palace Museum, it reveals certain higher-level commitments within the heritage sector. For a giant such as the Palace Museum to be versatile and innovative requires a high level of strategy.

In 2017, the museum launched the "Creative Laboratory" cooperation with the Tencent. The firm is not only a tech IT giant, but also the largest investment firm in the world and maker of the WeChat social media app, which combines the functions of Facebook, WhatsApp, Uber, Uber Eats, and Apple Wallet in one convenient app. WeChat is used by 938 million users in China and is quickly becoming the default mode of communication. Tencent helped the Palace Museum explore digital technologies for preserving, researching, and displaying cultural artifacts, to provide smart solutions and technological support for preserving national heritage while at the same time providing immersive experiences for visitors. Visitors can, for example, take a selfie and see how they would look dressed in Qing-dynasty costumes on an LED screen or see artifacts come to life though the use of augmented reality (AR) and mobile phone apps. Another initiative, "Next Idea," encouraged young technologists and designers to use the intellectual properties of Palace Museum to create emoticons, games, and comic strips. This is significant in that previously Chinese museums tended to be more guarded about sharing their IP, and certainly not interested in sharing it in such populist, informal ways.

In September of last year, Tencent launched a mobile AR app, Museum Officer, which is now in use at 100 museums, helping users all over China navigate the museum floor plans and their relevant exhibits. The Palace Museum is working hard to "distribute" its resources and its brand, and this app is the fruit of their ambitions.

Creating Cultural Destinations with Visitor Appeal

The idea that "social progress and development always rely on reform and innovation" has become a semiofficial mantra in China—innovation has been embraced as a national strategy, and its importance is very often reinforced from the highest positions in the state.[8] Institutions compete fiercely for the Most Innovative Museums Award, organized by the CMA. In 2014, the winner was the giant Nanjing Museum complex[9] with six main galleries and a temporary exhibition gallery, including one gallery focusing on intangible heritage that reopened in 2013. The Nanjing Museum claims to be more than a mere museum, espousing a much broader definition of the term, with exhibition events and festivals that create a vibrant atmosphere. The museum takes an "entertaining" approach to depicting life in the 1930s in its popular Republican Gallery, where authentic items from the Republican Era have been quite successfully incorporated into dioramas and where cafés, bookstores, and a theater are places of real consumption of cultural offerings. "Authentic items are incorporated in the set scenes, memories brought into reality, so that the exhibition turns into a participative experience," explains vice director Wang Qizhi. "Visitors can walk into a retro coffeehouse and have a real cup of coffee, walk into a variety shop and buy some rouge, or walk into a bookstore and flip through old books for a while."[10] Meanwhile the Digital Gallery allows visitors to step into an ancient Nanjing scene, which is projected on the wall. In the wall are a series of doors that visitors are encouraged to open. Each door reveals a different animated scene such as a waiter delivering food in a teahouse or a peasant woman winnowing rice. Many of the digital interactives also involve problem solving where visitors need to solve a puzzle to learn about the interior structure of an ancient vessel, or even play a video game that allows them to engage in techniques of ancient warfare. Beyond these interactives, the museum also encourages viewers to interact in a public and communal way by using a QR code to post their comments and photos.

The Nanjing Museum has a special understanding of history given that the city was such an important location during many historical eras. It was not only the capital of several dynasties throughout history but was also the government seat of the Republic of China (1912–1949). The city is probably most well known in the West as the site of the Nanjing Massacre (Rape of Nanking)—a tragedy that is addressed in a memorial hall dedicated to the subject.

The Nanjing Museum certainly has no small burden of history to process, and perhaps fittingly it is the first large, national, comprehensive museum in China. Given its wealth of experience, the museum exercises a great influence on other institutions throughout China, acting as a benchmark.

Housed in two palaces in a re-creation of Liao dynasty architecture,[11] the museum is spread between two buildings. This is no accident; Chinese museums seem to appreciate the importance of creating museum clusters in order to accommodate the large population and to create a travel-worthy destination. The extraordinarily-long history of the country, its cultural spirit, its size, and the imperial tradition seem to favor schemes—think the Forbidden City.

This tendency toward palaces of culture and grandiosity has been encouraged by China's rise to economic prosperity. Now with a very large proportion of wealthy billionaires, China has seen a boom in private museums. One of the most successful of these is a museum cluster outside of Chengdu, founded by businessman Fan Jianchuan in Anren Old Town. Said to be the largest private museum cluster in the world, the Jianchuan Museum Cluster received recognition by the by CMA as "China's Most Innovative Museum" in 2015. One of the few museums focusing mainly on the time period between the Anti-Japanese War (1937) and the end of the Cultural Revolution (1976), it has been praised for its courage to tackle this thorny period in Chinese history. Fan Jianchuan's motto, which is printed on a giant scaffold in the museum, is quietly critical: "To collect folklore for the sake of heritage; to collect lessons for the sake of the future; to collect war for the sake of peace; to collect disaster for the sake of tranquility."[12] The museum consists of 30 individual museums spread across 80 acres of land with a gross building area of over 100,000 square meters. Its collection of more than 8 million artifacts offers more than exhaustive coverage of the museum's four major themes: Anti-Japanese War (1937–1945), the "Red Age" (Cultural Revolution 1966–1976), the 2008 "Wenchuan earthquake," and "Folklore and Culture."[13] At least five of the 30 museums in the complex deal with politically sensitive subjects such as war, peace, and natural disasters, yet the interpretation causes little offense, as most is left to be constructed in the mind of the individual. Therefore, it avoids weighing in on the official political stance. For instance, Fan Jianchuan's "Museum of the Battlefield Front" offers little information on the battle, not to mention the protagonists or antagonists. (The hall actually refers to 22 very important Kuomintang battles.) The Museum of the Flying Tigers commemorates an alliance with the United States, exploring subjects such as the captives and civilian suffering, while some squares and monuments employ an artistic solution to present atypical treatments of certain topics.

Fan Jianchuan, as a private individual, had the benefit of starting from a blank slate, as he was not working from the "official templates" of state-owned museums. He thus envisioned his museum as something more within the realm of cultural industries with different kinds of retail, dining, and tourism functions such as teahouses, hotels, and antique shops.

The cluster, however, was not a completely private effort. In 2009, the Chengdu municipal government invested $820 million in making the small city of Anren near Chengdu (Dayi County, Sichuan Province) a heritage tourism destination—a push that, with the major private museum in existence, made Anren an attractive offer to tourists.[14] The very same year the CMA and the National Heritage Board granted the city the title of "Museum Town of China." Thus, the aim of the museum was, from the beginning, not only to serve the purposes of exhibition making, research, and education, but also, very purposefully, those of tourism as well. As China transitions from an economy based on agriculture and manufacturing to an economy with a rich mix of services, tourism has been an important way to spread wealth from the cities out to rural areas and from the East Coast to its interiors. Museums are a key part of this. Chengdu especially, once a city full of temples and storied teahouses, has bulldozed many of its attractions; thus, towns such as Anren are a big draw for day-trippers from Chengdu and domestic and international tourists traveling by coach and car.

With the success of towns such as Wuzhen and Anren also comes the question of cultural commodification. Will the "Ministry of Culture and National Tourism Administration," which was recently rebranded into a much-snappier "Ministry of Culture and Tourism" in April 2018,[15] further commodify culture, or will it democratize it both for national and international visitors? It is certainly an interesting perspective for the entire sector of "public memory" that was historically regarded as strictly nonprofit, entirely public, and usually scripted by official narratives.

Public Participation in Exhibition Content

Yinzhou District in Ningbo, like many "new districts" in China, is built on the ruins of a previously existing community, of mostly low-rise buildings. Ningbo Museum architect and Pritzker Prize winner Wang Shu lamented this destruction of community and context and thus decided to work with local artisans in building fragments of remaining brick into the beautifully textured façade of the building. Visiting the museum, one can see the date stamps on the actual bricks and the indents in the wall where both birds and plants now flourish. This attempt to seal wounds has been reflected in the programming of the museum, which makes admirable efforts to incorporate the public's views in the planning of their temporary exhibitions. With the tagline of "Citizen's Museum," the Ningbo Museum has moved their model of content creation from one that is supply driven (i.e., they create the

Figure 32 The Ningbo Museum (2008), designed by architect Wang Shu, was awarded the Pritzker Prize for outstanding forms and innovative techniques. The façade incorporates fragments of tile, brick, and cement from the surrounding neighborhoods, which were demolished to build the new CBD of Yingzhou in the East Coast city of Ningbo. Birds, plants, and mosses have also used the varied textures of the wall to create new habitats for themselves. *Photography: Chao Zhen. Photo courtesy: Chinese Museums Association Architecture and Technology Committee, China Archive of Museum Architecture, and the Nanjing Museum*

exhibitions and the public consumes them) to one that is demand driven (the public expresses their demands and the museum creates relevant exhibitions). Since 2010, they have been proactively conducting exit surveys, assisted by hundreds of volunteers (sometimes as many as 800 to 1,300 volunteers in the museum at one time) who approach visitors to learn about their likes and dislikes, to properly target the special exhibitions. Reviewing the language in the wall texts and providing contextual interpretive material along with accompanying events, the museum aids in bringing otherwise aloof, specialized content closer to the public, making logical improvements based on collected feedback.

The Future of Public Memory

This "public-facing" orientation can be seen elsewhere in the museum world in certain kinds of exhibition content that focus more on social histories over official narratives. In both official and nonofficial rhetoric, museums are being recognized as "public memory institutions." These are not the "glorious" memorial spaces adorned with banners and flowers, but rather the topics are more similar to public histories, which incorporate people's memories—both tangible and intangible—of both cultural experience and social change. This can be seen in the City Museum of Shenzhen, which includes both artifacts from and models of the workers in a construction barracks—exploring the lives of the young men who traveled so far from their homes to work in backbreaking construction sites.

This issue of public memory poses interesting questions for the trajectory of Chinese museums: Will the future take the form of a network of community-based museums that work on preserving, constructing, and exploring individual and collective memory? Or will the future take the form of a commodified memory organized into commercial cultural destinations? Perhaps it could be a balance of both or even some yet-to-be-discovered form that emerges from the bubbling stew of technology, local culture, and international innovations that characterizes daily life in contemporary China.

16

FROM INWARD-LOOKING TO OUTWARD-REACHING AND INTERNATIONAL MUSEUMS

Tian Kai

The emergence of museums in China, in the late 19th century, first took the form of foreign museums in treaty ports and territories such as Macao, Tianjin, and Shanghai. These colonial origins shroud the birth of museums in somewhat negative undertones. Despite the great benefits they brought, these museums were often characterized by mismatches and disconnects between the colonial elites and Chinese society as a whole. This process of exchange of culture would, throughout the history of Chinese museums, remain still somewhat fraught, but through these tensions, hybrid institutional forms emerged. Today, as you will find illustrated in this book, the cross-cultural dialogue between museums is characterized more by mutual enrichment.

Looking back, one of the core reasons for these initial disconnects is that most of the colonial museums were natural history museums, whereas Chinese collectors had generally focused more on antiquities. The Western botanists and zoologists used these museums (Shanghai Museum and Ziccawei Museum, also in Shanghai) for research but also to improve the overall level of scientific awareness within the public. During this time, China was characterized by conflicting forces and motivations toward both Western nations and their various ideologies and cultures.

On one hand, the May Fourth Movement represented a strong anti-imperialist sentiment that erupted when former German territories in Shandong were ceded to Japan through the Treaty of Versailles in 1919. A movement that started with 3,000 students in Beijing erupted around the country in general strikes and resulted with a minor

victory of Chinese officials abstaining from signing the Treaty of Versailles. Chinese citizens, having just escaped the yoke of feudalism, were not any longer keen to be controlled by foreign powers and made their concerns felt to the Republican government.

This movement, while resisting foreign occupation, nonetheless urged the adoption of foreign science, technology, and even values such as women's liberation and democracy. China's defeat in the Opium War, and the "Shandong problem," had many intellectuals feeling betrayed by the country's leaders and wondering if, in fact, perhaps their whole system was not at least a little broken. A group of thinkers represented by historian and geographer Wei Yuan blamed this defeat on a backwardness of the conservative ruling class and resistance to technology and new ideas. Wei Yuan proposed that the Chinese learn the most advanced technology of the "barbarians" in his famous phrase *weiyizhiyi* 以夷制夷 translated literally as "use the foreigners to control the foreigners" or more eloquently to "beat the foreigners at their own game." There was a general view that if Chinese officials had been more adept at international affairs and less focused on the machinations occurring within their own countries, they could have emerged from World War I in a much more advantageous position. This phrase, *weiyizhiyi*, is crucial in the understanding of the early history of Chinese museums and even today as institutions jockey for recognition and resources—the concept of being cognizant of the global landscape and sensitive to local conditions is vital to the success of Chinese museums.

Figure 33 Nantong Museum (1905, 1955), China's first modern museum founded by a Chinese national in 1905, features a newer building (pictured) completed in 1955. The buildings rest within a garden complex. Founder Zhang Jian envisioned the museum as a garden. It is referred to in Chinese as a *bowuyuan* rather than the commonly used *bowuguan*, the suffix *yuan* meaning garden, and *guan* meaning hall or building. *Photography: Chao Zhen. Photo courtesy: Chinese Museums Association Architecture and Technology Committee, China Archive of Museum Architecture, and the Nanjing Museum*

Zheng Guanying, a businessman and author of *Words of Warning to a Prosperous Age*, argued that the foundation of the wealth and strength of Western powers laid in technology, and rested upon a foundation of learning and a concerted focus on economic and industrial developments, more efficient legislation, and political reform. Zheng stressed practical learning over the focus on philosophy, history, and ethics that characterized traditional Chinese learning with its focus on classic and Confucian texts. He thought that in order to properly understand physics, one should learn from personal observation rather than rely on secondhand knowledge. He believed that a museum, where different objects are housed, helps improve the level of understanding of the public and acts to consolidate professional knowledge. But journalist and scholar Liang Qichao, one of the ardent reformers at the time, lamented that the early development of Chinese museums was marked by a lack of artifacts, let alone the other elements of a museum.

The year 1905 saw the establishment of the first museum founded by a Chinese national. The Nantong Museum, which was built and funded by the industrialist Zhang Jian, had the clear purpose of "preserving Chinese national culture and benefiting scholars," signifying the start of the development of locally built, locally operated museums, sometimes with unique Chinese characteristics.

The function and purpose of the museum continued to evolve and expand as we can see with the Henan Provincial Museum, established in 1927, which had elaborated on the mission statement of Nantong with four guiding principles:

1. To provide greater access to a larger number of people; to create awareness of existing culture.

2. To encourage academic research.

3. To increase the level of public knowledge.

4. To promote and facilitate social progress.

Social progress and the promotion of culture were the two most significant functions of Chinese museums at that time. The first exhibition at the Henan Museum in 1928 aimed to create a panorama of different ethnic groups or nationalities. The exhibition hall was filled with a large number of models and also pictures that illustrated the

Tian Kai

customs of various ethnic groups from around China and the world. The exhibition also included pictures of historical figures, the Three Sovereigns and Five Emperors—figures that are today considered mythical deities rather than concrete historical figures. What's interesting here is the kind of encyclopedic approach to ethnicity and rationalist regimentation of knowledge, combined with the inclusion of these mythical figures that predate even the Xia dynasty—China's first dynasty, but one that is also seen as a "mythical dynasty" lacking concrete evidence.[1]

Despite this mix of deities and humans in the exhibition, the Henan Museum was, however, quite forward-thinking and modern in terms of governance, setting up a board of trustees consisting of scholars, presidents of universities, officials, prominent personalities, and museum staff. These systems of governance were in fact somewhat common in the first half of the 20th century with the boards of the Palace Museum, Nanjing Museum, and Henan Museum being nominated to weigh in on important institutional decisions.

Since the museum was still in its infancy, the exhibition, which contained mostly metal and stone objects, was not arranged in a systematic fashion. The conditions at that time were such that many exhibitions did not always provide the best educational opportunities for viewers.

Outlined below are some of the issues: First, modern historiography was not well developed in China at that time. Scholars led by Liang Qichao, the father of modern historiography, advocated "new historiography," which led to the beginning of a modern historical consciousness. His text "New Historiography" was a call for Chinese historians to understand their nation in a global context—a history that focused not on court annals, emperors, and dynasties but on a history of the state, groups, and facts more than ideals or moral principles. It rejected the narrative flourish of history, the cult of personality that led to the mythologization of emperors; rather it saw historical figures as actors within different historical stages rather than ancient celebrities.

Second, archaeology had also not yet fully come into its own in the early 20th century, because its connection with historiography was not well established, although historiography and archaeology started to become more aligned in 1921. Third, the role of the museum was still in the process of being defined.

As the decades rolled on, these ideas were further refined, but soon China began to enter into the Soviet orbit, which also changed how museums were defined. Since 1949, the concept of "social engagement" in China centered on Socialist notions of social transformation and social engineering. The first national meeting of museums, held in May 1956, defined the museum as an institute for research and education and a major repository for tangible and intangible cultural heritage and natural specimens.

This definition provided fundamental guidelines for all museum-related work. Mao also threw his support behind the museum in 1958; while on an inspection tour of the Anhui Museum he proclaimed, "There should be museums like this in the major cities of every province because it is important for people to have a good knowledge of their own history and to know the power of creativity." Since then, the government set out to establish museums in each province of China, which focused on local historical narratives. Many of these museums used the 1959 exhibition "China General History Exhibition" (The National Museum of Chinese History) as a template applying this format to their own local histories. These exhibitions highlighted the integration of regional histories into China's history as a whole and were framed by Marxist notions of dialectical and historical materialism. Rather than emperors or dynasties, humans became the key agents of history, and class struggle became the central conflict. Instead of focusing solely on the emperors and court officials, museums turned their sights on the working classes—"laborers" now became key roles in the story.

Concepts of history and culture in the early 20th century were still in an embryonic stage, and thus the stories told by museums in the 1910s, 1920s, and 1930s tended to be vague, allowing for a miscellany of objects to be deemed as either culturally or historically significant. It wasn't until the 1950s that the museums began to take interest in the history of working people—in recognizing their value in society, with a similar direction to "social history" in the West (which rose to prominence in the 1960s) but different presentation in terms of exhibition form.

Other elements of Soviet influence included the establishment of Friends of the Museum (FoM) organizations (in Shaanxi and Jiangsu Provinces), which assisted the museum in collecting artifacts and launching publicity campaigns. These organizations, however, were disbanded during the Cultural Revolution. This retreat into stiff, inward-looking institutions understandably resulted in less social engagement. During this conservative era, innovation was not rewarded; museums were largely identical and seldom visited.

In 1979, during the early days of the Reform and Opening-Up, museums emerged from their seclusion; the National Cultural Heritage Administration (NCHA) stated that museums "shall hold lectures, coordinate with schools in teaching, compile publicity brochures, organize mobile exhibitions, and make stronger efforts to make scientific knowledge accessible to a greater number of people."

FoM associations were also resumed in order to create a better connection between "the collection [and] the general public." With the regulations to protect their existence, FoMs were established or restored in places like Shanghai, Hunan, Jiangsu, and Henan. Shanghai Museum even expanded the presence of its FoM association overseas with two aims: first, to enable the purchase of artifacts from overseas, and second, to raise money for a new building.

Some of the most forward-thinking approaches to outreach and education would come out of Harbin, with the Northeast China Revolutionary Martyrs Memorial Hall, dubbed "the light-infantry of the museum front" due to its efforts to organize mobile exhibitions in factories, schools, and military camps as early as 1977. Some museums even began to purchase video cameras and projectors in an effort to offer lessons to the public electronically.

The Chinese museum world began to really gather momentum in the 1980s, as we began to see a spate of modernized museums reopening to the public, including Shaanxi Museum of History, the Shanghai Museum, and the Henan Museum. They not only possessed new buildings and equipment but also had fundamental shifts in management. In 1987, Shaanxi political leader Han Yong proposed that certain museum services should be outsourced, such as cleaning, building maintenance, and security, which were usually given to private firms or property management companies. The 1980s and 1990s also saw the introduction of computerized management systems; for instance, the Shaanxi Museum of History computerized its collection and books and even its administration when it moved to its new location in 1991. Keeping with their progressive march toward the goal of outreach, a number of museums in Beijing—National Museum of Chinese History, Beijing Museum of Natural History, and the Beijing Planetarium—launched their own websites, extending the depth and breadth to their audiences.

This push toward a people-forward institution was substantially aided by political leader Li Changchun (a member of Politburo Standing Committee), who on a visit to the Henan Museum proclaimed that museums should work to create a strong bond with regular people. This became a milestone, and Henan Museum became a test case for how this ideology might manifest itself within the institution.

The museum began by upgrading its exhibitions, client services, and scientific research, making the principle of "people first" applicable to every task within the museum and thus using this mission statement to completely reform the museum's policies and practices. This pilot project was deemed a success and soon began to spread to other parts of the country.

With new models being tested out, the State Administration of Culture and Heritage was interested in how it might promote different kinds of "excellence" and encourage the museums who were lagging behind. In 2008, it launched a ranking system for national and first-class museums, which assessed the *impact* of the museum on society using criteria such as its organization and management of exhibitions, procurement of resources, and level of community engagement. This system brought about a sharp rise in the quantity and quality of exhibitions on show, and some museums began to explore the curatorial system, making the creation of unique exhibitions the goal of the museum along with a diverse array of public-oriented educational events.

To this end, Shanghai Museum set up more than 40 educational bases in schools in Shanghai, establishing, "Textbook Courses," "Study Groups," and "Schoolyard Exhibitions." In Beijing, the National Museum, in collaboration with Shijia Primary School, developed "The Roaming National Museum: A Course for Shijia Primary School," a project in which textbooks covering topics such as characters, clothing, utensils, and aesthetics were developed in conjunction with the museum's collections. Many of these programs, such as the Henan Museum initiative, were the products of negotiation, codesign, and collaboration between different schools and museums, and they can be found in a book compiled by the Chinese Museum Association (CMA) titled *Selected Excellent Cases of Education Programs of China's Museums*, which includes 43 examples of compelling educational material.

Though all of these measures go a distance toward outreach, social engagement in its truest sense cannot be achieved without the introduction of societal elements into the management structure through the introduction of boards of trustees. Though many museums already had actively functioning boards, those who didn't were officially mandated to set them up by NCHA in the 2015 "Guidance on the Establishment of the Board of Trustees"—a policy that was followed by pilot programs and guidance for implementation across the country.

In 2011, Shan Jixiang, then director of NCHA, in his book *Walled House to the Outside World: Thoughts on the Museum in Its Broader Sense*, wrote, "The exhibition sites are now not inside the museum, but within the communities, from the cities to the rural areas, from above ground to below ground, from inside the country to outside of it. When thinking of museums in the broader sense of culture and heritage, we learn that museums are committed to an outward-looking strategy, promoting social progress and meeting the public's needs on multiple dimensions. This new view of museums puts public needs at its core and helps museums keep up with the times."

17

THE V&A'S PARTNERSHIP WITH THE DESIGN SOCIETY IN SHENZHEN

An Ongoing Legacy of Cultural Diplomacy

Tim Reeve

On a sunny December morning in 2017, overlooking Shenzhen Bay from the reclaimed land of the Shekou peninsula, the Sea World Culture and Arts Centre (SWCAC)—the new home of Design Society, China's first platform dedicated to design—opened its doors to the world. It was designed to be the cultural heart of the type of large-scale retail, commercial, and residential development so commonplace in modern China, with China Merchants Shekou Industrial Zone Holdings (CMSK) as the client—the holder of exclusive development rights to the area since the creation of the Shekou Industrial Zone in 1979. The architect of SWCAC was Japan's celebrated Pritzker Prize winner, Fumihiko Maki. He was invited in 2011 to undertake his first project in China, with a brief to respond to the coastal location and the beautiful views of the mountains of Hong Kong in creating a complex for a variety of cultural activities, including museums, gallery spaces, a lecture theater, grand function hall, and a private art gallery, along with a diverse and complementary range of retail and leisure spaces.

The form of the building responds to its context with three huge boxes protruding toward the natural features that surround it: the ocean to the south, the adjacent park, and the mountains to the north. Inside, the array of spaces—large and small—across six floors (including a subterranean carpark and roof garden), totaling 70,000 square meters, branch off a vast and welcoming day-lit atrium with light flooding in from all sides. The first gallery space visitors encounter is the V&A Gallery of Design, curated by London's Victoria and Albert Museum, along with China Merchants, the founding partner of Design Society.

The question I have been asked most often about the V&A's new gallery is, why China? The question is typically followed by a comment about the rapid expansion of museums since the millennium—a new museum opening every week, or one a day during the most intensive phases, usually on the back of major real estate developments—and that if you were to visit one of them, the chances are you could have it all to yourself. This might be enough to make any museum, with an international reputation to protect, think twice before engaging in such a rapidly expanding environment. And yet in 2014, the V&A—a publicly funded UK museum—entered into a five-year contract with China Merchants, Shekou—a giant Chinese state-owned company (of similar age to the V&A) specializing originally in transportation, and now with major interests in global logistics, urban development, healthcare, insurance, and banking.

So why take on such an ambitious project so far from home? The V&A is widely recognized as the world's leading museum of art, design, and performance—a treasure trove of knowledge and museological expertise, housing a world-class collection of over 2.3 million objects and 19 national collections—spanning 5,000 years of human creativity and ingenuity from around the globe. The V&A also possesses an international reputation for groundbreaking, immersive, and performative exhibition-making, the largest lender of objects of any British museum within the United Kingdom, and an audience that continues to grow and to diversify.

For the beginnings of an answer, we need to go back to the origin of the V&A, and even before. The seeds of the V&A's creation—and also of the notion of the economic and cultural importance of what we now call the creative industries in the United Kingdom—were sown in the design school

Figure 34 "Craft: The Reset," at Design Society. Jian Huang's "Umbrella Pavilion III," paper and bamboo, 2018, explores how traditional techniques can be repurposed to create new forms. *Photography: Huang Mingjian. Photo courtesy: Design Society*

Figure 35 "BENDING RULES," Prof. Kristof Crolla, aluminum, metal tubes, 2018. This installation shows a continuation of the research conducted for the ZCB Bamboo Pavilion. The aluminum tubes represent the bamboo and bend in a similar way. *Photography: Huang Mingjian. Photo courtesy: Design Society*

movement of the first half of the 19th century. Design education is where our story began, and design education and inspiration for the artists and designers of today and tomorrow is what drives our mission today, whether through our development initiative titled "FuturePlan" at the V&A in South Kensington, at the Museum of Childhood in Bethnal Green, through the creation of the recently opened design museum in Dundee, Scotland, or as the founding partner in the creation of China's first institution dedicated to design in the heartland of China's growing creative economy.

Inspiration also comes from the fact that, although the V&A has always been a local and national museum, it has also always been international, with a global outlook from its very inception. There is a large oil painting in the V&A's collection, by the English painter Henry Selous, that captures the opening of the Great Exhibition—the first World's Fair—in London in 1851, where exhibitors came from across the globe to showcase the best of technology, design, and artistry. In the foreground, standing proudly at the front of a small crowd of commissioners, ministers, and foreign dignitaries surrounding Queen Victoria and the royal family, is the painting's most intriguing figure. His identity is not certain, because although he is wearing traditional Chinese dress, no formal representative of the Chinese government is recorded as attending the Great Exhibition. It has recently been suggested that he is Mr. Xisheng, a mariner who arrived in England some months before the Great Exhibition on board the *Keying*—the first Chinese ship to enter British waters. He was invited to attend the opening of the Great Exhibition as an informal representative of the Manchu government, after Queen Victoria herself boarded his ship to congratulate him. The V&A was founded shortly after this moment, using the proceeds and inspiration of the Great Exhibition to build a collection and to open the South Kensington Museum in 1857. It is a somewhat romantic tale perhaps, but from its inception, the painting has the V&A facing outward to the world, and as this chance encounter between Queen Victoria and a Chinese adventurer was taking place, the United Kingdom was engaged in creative exchange and cultural diplomacy with China, with the V&A at the vanguard.

The V&A acquired its first Chinese objects in 1852 and is now the proud custodian of one of the most comprehensive collections of Chinese art and design outside East Asia. From 3000 BC to the present day, the collection comprises over 18,000 artifacts, including ceramics, jade, metalwork, lacquer, textiles, furniture, sculpture, bamboo, glass, paintings, manuscripts, and prints. Collecting to inspire artists and designers in the rich traditions of Chinese craftsmanship was one of the cornerstones of the new institution, but well beyond the newly constructed edifice of the V&A, the Arts and Crafts Movement—a global aesthetic phenomenon pioneered in 19th-century

Britain—greatly inspired by Chinese art, was creating a powerful cultural link between our two nations. Some 165 years later, the V&A curated the seminal "China Design Now" exhibition to coincide with the Beijing Olympics, and in 2013, the celebrated Chinese artist Xu Bing transformed the V&A's John Madejski Garden with a magical installation, "Travelling to the Wonderland," inspired by the classic Chinese fable Taohua Yuan Ji (The Peach Blossom Spring), as part of the "Masterpieces of Chinese Painting 700–1900" exhibition, October 26, 2013–January 19, 2014. The cultural relationship between China and the V&A is as old as the museum itself, strengthened through decades of research, knowledge exchange, and collaboration. And increasingly, curatorial relationships are inspiring political and economic dialogue between China and the United Kingdom, with successive prime ministers describing the importance of our strategic partnership as "a golden era of relations between China and the UK."

So, many decades after the founding of the V&A, the opening of its most ambitious overseas partnership should be seen as the latest chapter in a much longer narrative, and as an extraordinary opportunity to renew and deepen our engagement with China, at a key moment in its history. Just as the V&A was founded when London was experiencing a boom in manufacturing, innovation, and design during the Industrial Revolution, today a similar design revolution is taking place in Shenzhen—the fastest-growing design city in the world. Just like London, Shenzhen and the Pearl River Delta, with its megacity population almost the size of the United Kingdom's, is increasingly driven by its creative industries. It is fast outgrowing its "factory of the world" label—as a center of manufacturing—transitioning to a center of design and attracting the most ambitious designers from China and around the world in the process. Many objects we use every day are now no longer just "made in China," they are also "designed in China"—by enterprising young creatives working with innovative new materials and techniques. The short answer to "Why China?" can be found here in dizzying Technicolor.

The V&A's collaboration with CMSK represents a new model for museums to extend their mission and brand to new audiences. It is genuinely pioneering, the first between a major UK museum and a Chinese state-owned enterprise. Twenty years on from the opening of the Guggenheim Bilbao, the Louvre Abu Dhabi opened with a particularly ambitious and uncompromising statement of intent in Jean Nouvel's dreamy new building on Saadiyat Island in the Arabian peninsula, just a few weeks before Design Society. Both represent confident deployments of cultural capital by world-leading museums, and investments in bricks and mortar for the long term. But for the V&A, this partnership offered an opportunity to engage with the Shenzhen creative community in creating and curating a new design gallery, freed up from the responsibilities of commissioning, designing, funding, and constructing a new building, with its ongoing operational responsibilities, focusing instead on advice, training, and content development. As well as the V&A Gallery, the V&A has provided a wide range of museum consultancy to share 165 years of insight and know-how with Design Society, in our role as its founding partner. Together with a range of partners in Shenzhen, we were able to develop a comprehensive learning and engagement program with a network of schools, universities, start-ups, and more established design and technology companies. This has helped to inform an audience engagement plan that will ensure the impact of Design Society is felt by real people for many years to come, and at the same time provided the inspiration for the first exhibition in the V&A Gallery—"Values of Design."

As soon as the contracts were signed in 2014, in the Foreign and Commonwealth Office in London as part of Premier Li Keqiang's visit, the V&A created a small, dedicated team to work in Shenzhen, including the secondment of Dr. Luisa Mengoni, a senior curator from the Asia Department, to work closely with the fast-moving and burgeoning creative community during a 3-year research phase, developing new networks and researching the concept for the new V&A Gallery. We were determined from the outset that our model would not see the V&A exporting content to China, but rather would involve the V&A creating a narrative informed by Shenzhen and the Pearl River Delta. In a sense, it would use its collections and new acquisitions—including the first museum acquisition of a social media platform, WeChat (including original sketches for the WeChat emoticon "Bubble Pup" and, for display both at the V&A and then at Design Society, 2 demo APK files of WeChat for the Android operating system, both offline versions of the software) through our partnership with Tencent in Guangzhou—to hold a mirror up to Chinese contemporary design practice. A clear example of this engagement saw the V&A's Shekou team present "Unidentified Acts of Design" at the 2015 Shenzhen Urbanism Architecture Bi-City Biennale, with displays exploring eight stories about design and production in the Pearl River Delta. It was initiated as a pilot project to help us explore more thoroughly Shenzhen's design and production landscape, to inform the V&A Gallery.

The output of this research was "Values of Design"—the inaugural exhibition in Design Society—telling a story of international design from the 20th to the 21st century, in a way that reflects and is relevant to contemporary Chinese design practice. Some 250 objects from the V&A's collections, from 31 different countries and assembled over the course of 160 years, are imaginatively displayed alongside 45 new V&A objects acquired from Shenzhen's studios and factories in the period before opening. It was conceived as a broad exploration of the relationship between ideas of values and design, which are of particular importance and relevance in such a fast-moving and sometimes chaotic context. By identifying several key values that have been driving design processes around the world across the past two centuries, the objects in the exhibition either support or question these value claims, triggering the audience to reflect on how they themselves value design.

As well as considering how values drive design, the exhibition highlights the key role that design plays in society and showcases objects that represent key turning points in the history of design against the backdrop of Shenzhen, a city in which design and manufacturing are developing at a rapid rate. In the context of contemporary China, the term "design" has taken on many different values, from personal expression and problem solving to economic development.

The seven themes providing the narrative framework represent broad value statements made about design in the past: performance, cost, problem-solving, materials, identity, communication, and wonder. The geographic and historical range of objects on display creates new associations that highlight the common design values that shape different objects from around the world. For instance, a 17th-century Iranian astrolabe and a contemporary Swiss Army knife are paired to highlight the human need or instinct to combine multiple functions into a single object. Nineteenth-century silk shoes, a paper dress from the 1960s, and a Stella McCartney H&M jumpsuit place the value of low-cost design in a longer historical context. Issues and values that we often mistake as being unique to the modern world are shown to have a historical precedent from which we can learn, or at least react.

There are many lessons to draw from our time in and around Shenzhen, and our partnership with China Merchants, but the opportunity to work so closely and intensively with Chinese practitioners from a range of creative disciplines has been thrilling and rewarding beyond measure. The memory of idiosyncratic Chinese import regulations, or the complexities of the onshore and offshore tax framework, while maddening and seemingly insurmountable during the contract development and negotiations, are now just a distant memory. The contract has stayed where all good contracts remain, locked away in a filing cabinet.

The Values of Design gallery, curated by Brendan Cormier and Luisa Mengoni and designed by Sam Jacob Studio, is the most tangible and visible legacy of the V&A at Design Society. But it is the engagement of people from all walks of life beyond its walls, the networks developed around its creation, and the thousands of young Chinese people who will seek inspiration there, and use their imagination and ingenuity to drive the creative economy of the future, that will endure.

The torch has, in a sense, been picked up by CMSK's own team of professional curators, including director Ole Bouman, Dutch curator, critic, and historian and former founder of *Archis* magazine, *Volume* magazine, and the Netherlands Architecture Institute. Bouman's engagement in the region began in 2013, when he was appointed chief curator of the "Urbanism/Architecture Bi-City Biennale of Shenzhen/Hong Kong"—a biennale that explores urbanism and urbanization in the context of the Pearl River Delta, using former industrial facilities in Shekou as venues.

The curatorial team looks at design through the lens of Shenzhen and its innovators but also takes a broader look back at China's rich legacy of design, which was so sophisticated that in the 15th century all of Europe was clamoring for its products. The most recent exhibition, "Craft: The Reset," showcases designers using traditional methods—for instance, Chinese paper umbrella making techniques—and applying them to the creation of modern furniture. But beyond this dialogue between tradition and innovation, the exhibition sometimes takes a "meta" perspective. For instance, Huo Yijin's installation of porcelain vases titled "Sky Blue" touches on the ecological impact of porcelain production, which requires large kilns burning at high temperatures. Yet these somewhat sobering themes are balanced by lighter, more aesthetically driven pieces, complemented by light, almost ebullient, exhibition design. The pieces are displayed in an open, multiperspectival environment that seems unafraid to show its seams. This transparency of "surface" and "structure," "front" and "back," makes it so that exhibition design itself becomes an artifact speaking to the themes of the exhibition.

At a time when the UK creative and knowledge economy is in such robust health, and with the post-Brexit landscape placing a renewed emphasis on international trade for UK companies and institutions, we are grateful for the opportunity to take a role in inspiring different approaches to exhibition making and cultural collaboration. For the V&A's international strategy, there is a flexibility, responsiveness, relevance, pace, and tactical opportunism in our approach that feels close to our founding mission. The V&A is at its best when it is innovating and experimenting, and where it leaves itself space to do so by not locking itself into the responsibilities of bricks and mortar and long-term contracts. Being prepared to take our collections and ideas to new and surprising places and connecting with audiences that may not otherwise engage with the V&A, is part of what makes our international work distinctive.

PART IV:
CASE STUDIES IN INNOVATION

18

PALACE MUSEUM

Museum Fever—Keeping Up with Public Demands for New Experiences

Shan Jixiang

In September 2015, the Palace Museum had the fortunate problem of being faced with a veritable stampede of visitors. Given the overwhelming response to the exhibition "The Precious Collection of the Stone Moat," the museum had to employ extra staff to manage the hundreds of people queued first *outside* the museum then *inside* the exhibition to urge viewers along. Outside, visitors waited for more than 9 or 10 hours, arriving as early as 5 a.m. with folding chairs and snacks, waiting to get a glimpse of 12th-century scroll "Along the River at Qingming Festival." This phenomenon became known as *gugong pao* or "Storming the Palace."

We expect this length of queue for major box-office hits or the latest model of iPhone, but recently China has seen a surging popularity in antiquities and traditional culture, a kind of "museum fever." In 2017, another special exhibition, "A Panorama of Rivers and Mountains: Blue-Green Landscape Paintings from Chinese History," re-created the "run on the palace" as viewers flocked to see the masterpiece of the same name by Wang Ximeng. Staff had to limit the crowds to 30-minute slots and allowed only 150 viewers in at a time, capping the total daily visitors to 2,400. The museum staff put in extensive overtime, extending the museum hours to deal with the mass popularity of the exhibit, even offering bottled water and instant noodles to the patient lines of visitors.[1]

This "fever" seemed to spread to other institutions—the Capital Museum's exhibition "Splendid Finds: The Archaeological Excavations of Haihunhou Kingdom," which displayed treasures from the most well-preserved Han Dy-

nasty Tomb, created a run of its own. Among the collection of ancient distilling vessels and a large collection of bells, visitors were delighted to find an ancient hotpot vessel—an interesting discovery in that the nobles were not thought to enjoy this simple dish, now eagerly consumed in every corner of the country, known abroad as "fondue chinois" or "steamboat." Another exhibition, "Queen, Mother, General: 40th Anniversary of the Excavation of the Shang Tomb of Fu Hao," featuring artifacts from the tomb of legendary queen and warrior Fu Hao, led to a second run on the Capital Museum. This pattern repeated itself all over China, at the National Museum (Beijing), the Shanghai Museum, and the Nanjing Museum—each attracting its own long queue of visitors. Fueled by a revival in *guoxue*—the study of Chinese traditional culture—supported by the Chinese government—this museum fever seems to imply that queuing for a museum has become a new kind of secular ritual signaling one's interest in and devotion to national culture. This movement has been stimulated by Xi Jinping, making culture and museums a national priority.

Creating a Dynamic Culture of Teaching and Research

While it is important to create meaningful experiences for the public, rigorous research is not only inherently important, but it can be the basis of unique exhibition narratives. Research needs to form the backbone of the museum, but preservation is also vital in order to guarantee well-preserved collections for future generations of researchers. Beyond its existing plans for maintenance and preservation, the Forbidden City has implemented a new plan from

2020 to 2035 in order to secure the sustainability of the Palace Museum for the next 600 years.

The Palace Museum has also established the Palace Museum Relics Hospital, which is devoted to the use of science and technology in terms of heritage and artifact preservation. Completed in 2016, the relic hospital is the largest of its kind, with a comprehensive array of functions, research facilities, and the largest number of professional staff of any other similar institution. The Relic Hospital is also home to the International Training Center for Conservation of the International Institute for the Conservation of Historic and Artistic Works. The Relic Hospital carries out technological restoration and routine maintenance on collections of relics supporting institutions in China and around the world.

The work of the training center is supported by the research of the Palace Museum Institute for Archaeology, founded in 2013, which encompasses 20 departments with experts and scholars in related fields building on the museum's networks both in China and abroad. This cutting-edge research institution takes an egalitarian approach to research, being both institutionally open and focused on talent development.

With the Forbidden City in its backyard, the Palace Museum makes for an excellent training base. To date the museum has completed 27 research and excavation projects in the Forbidden City, including Ming and Qing structures, the Hall of Great Profundity, and the Southern Warehouses, where discarded and broken imperial porcelain and jade implements were kept, a kind of "elite" pottery dump, away from the hands of commoners. Outside the Forbidden City, the team was involved in other excavations, such as the Jingdezhen imperial kilns, and the site of an ancient port at Kollam in Kerala, India, where dredging of the port unearthed shards of local Indian pottery, Mediterranean glasswares, and Tang dynasty coins.

Interinstitutional Collaborations

In 2016 China's museums hosted a total of 30,800 exhibitions; however, only a few museums were able to create the same level of buzz and dedicated queuing. Some museums still struggle to retain visitors, and the high-quality museums and exhibitions tend to be concentrated in certain cities. There are still huge imbalances between the east coast and the interior, and between urban and rural areas. Enhanced intermuseum and regional cooperation can help alleviate these disparities through resource sharing and personnel exchanges.

The Palace Museum has also been sharing the wealth of its collection with other institutions around the country.

We have maintained long-term, fruitful relationships with museums and institutions such as the Capital Museum, Shanghai Museum, Suzhou Museum, Hong Kong Leisure and Cultural Services Department, and the Macao Museum of Art.

But beyond merely lending exhibitions, the Palace Museum has been cooperating with institutions in greater China to build exhibition galleries; for instance, the Kulangsu Gallery of Foreign Artefacts from the Palace Museum Collection, created as a cooperation with the Xiamen Municipal Government, and another agreement with the Hong Kong West Kowloon Cultural District Authority for a Hong Kong branch of the Palace Museum—7,600 square meters of antiquities housed in a space designed by Rocco Architects, the designers of the Guangdong Museum.

IP and Merchandizing Collaborations

Following government directives for museums to monetize their cultural assets, the Palace Museum has engaged in a number of collaborations, including the Palace Museum Workshop for Huizhou Traditional Craftsmanship in the city of Huangshan, in Anhui Province. The project aims to sustain and support traditions of Huizhou craftsmanship and upgrade the Huizhou traditional arts and crafts brand through innovation. Another example is the recent establishment of the Cultural Innovation Center of the Palace Museum in Pingyao, Shanxi Province. The center aims to work on the creation and development of products and merchandise. The Palace Museum will share its wealth of experience, having created over 9,600 products of its own with an annual revenue from sales of souvenirs of over 1 billion RMB.

The Palace Museum is also making an effort to spread its professional knowledge through the Gugong Institute, which has set up branches in seven cities, including Shanghai, Huizhou, Shenzhen, and Xiamen. These institutes provide opportunities for residents and tourists not only to buy the museum's merchandise but take part in lectures on topics such as the influence of Yangtze River Delta craftsmen on the construction of the Forbidden City. The institute also offers a number of training courses on topics such as restoration, painting, porcelain appraisal, and management.

Digital Outreach Makes Heritage Consumption an Everyday Habit

Moving away from the quiet, sleepy model of the past, when exhibits appealed to only a small group of researchers, the Palace Museum now produces digital content to bring artifacts to life. Through strategic partnerships with digital content providers, we have learned not only new ways to tell these stories but also methods to help disseminate them to a greater public. One of our most wide-reaching achievements was the 2017 TV program *National Treasure*, which introduced the various select and unique artifacts to a general audience. Nine national museums, including the Palace Museum, cooperated with China Central Television (CCTV) to launch this effort, aimed at extending the reach of the museum to the distant regions of China. The program attracted over 800 million viewers through traditional television networks, 20 million through online streaming platform Bilibili, and 400 million views on Weibo (Chinese Twitter). This initiative shows how museums can collaborate with traditional media to not only extend their outreach but produce one of the most popular history programs in the country. *National Treasure* was actually shown beyond Chinese borders, debuting on the main stage of the Cannes MIPTV Media Festival—an incubator and content-buying market that helps link up producers, buyers, financers, and distributors. Beyond its value as outreach, this endeavor actually spurred a noticeable jump in museum viewership—the average visits of the nine national museums increased by 50 percent, compared to the previous year.

Another example of this kind of collaboration between museums and media outlets was the 100-episode documentary "Every Treasure Tells a Story," jointly produced by the National Cultural Heritage Administration and CCTV. This program told the stories of 100 national treasures—in five-minute, casually narrated episodes—offering a video index of Chinese civilization that could be easily consumed by mobile phone users during their daily commutes. Both television series employed high production values, animations, and sometimes a quirky visual language to make these ancient relics appeal to a younger demographic.

The museum has also extended its outreach through an extensive variety of apps; over ten apps are now available on the app store. The goal of these apps is not to act so much as a guide to the in-situ museum experience but to provide different kinds of experiences of the material for different kinds of visitors both inside and outside the museum.

For the visitor with a casual interest in the aesthetics of the collection, the museum has created an elegant calendar app—356 Masterpieces—with luscious images of the objects in the collection. For those interested in fashion, the Qing Emperor's Wardrobe App features 3D scans of the emperor's various garments. The Night Revels of Han Xizai! gives us a deeper look into the life of a failing emperor, who loses himself in artistic pursuits as his empire crumbles around him. Meanwhile, Twelve Beauties of Prince Yong uses the "Chinese Beauty" genre of court painting to explore some of the more idiosyncratic elements of the collection of the Palace Museum. Emperor for a Day uses

Figure 37 Screenshot from 1 of 10 apps developed by the Palace Museum (Beijing) partnered with technology firm Tencent to enable visitors to explore the museum in different ways, including calendar apps, games, and social connections with Palace Museum fans. *Photo courtesy: Rebecca Catching*

the character of a small child and his lion cub sidekick to create an interactive experience of bounding through the palace. Finally, the Palace Museum Community is aimed at addressing the social needs of museumgoers through a platform similar to Sim Life, where viewers can explore the space of the museum and its services and offerings, but they can also create their own space and interact with neighbors in a virtual Forbidden City.

Advertisement for the Palace Community App

The Palace Museum is also very forward-thinking in designing new digital interactives within the museum space to capitalize on our most popular objects, ones that might not stand up well to repeated exposure. In May of 2018, we launched the digital version of the 12th-century scroll

"Along the River at Qingming Festival." Visitors can "get on the boat" to discover the details hidden within this extremely intricate painting, which are often not easily visible through the original work.

These attempts at digital outreach not only provide fantastic learning opportunities but are a great way to present research conducted in the "back of house" to those at the "front of house"—thus uniting the two functions of the museum to conduct a high standard of research and at the same time remain public-facing and well adapted to the changing attitudes and tastes of viewers. Today's visitors have different needs; they not only want access to "handheld" museums via mobile phone and tablet platforms that can be perused while lying lazily on the couch, but they also want to sustain their lifelong learning and meet friends who share the same interests. The Palace Museum makes it our goal to facilitate that.

Figure 38 The Palace Museum received more than 29 million visitors in 2018. *Photo courtesy: Qi Mengbo.*

19

SHANGHAI MUSEUM

"A History of the World in 100 Objects"—Growing a Capacity for Institutional Change

Yang Zhigang

As most English language readers will know, changing museums is a daunting task in any culture. Why? Museums are complex institutions that are not generally well understood. Deep understanding can be achieved through consistent exploration by curators and museum professionals with hands-on experience, and by people who are in constant dialogue with the public, soliciting their reactions and interpretations. In this regard, social media platforms like WeChat can be enormously helpful. The 2008 free-admission policy greatly improved our efforts at audience research, given the sheer volume of visitors from different backgrounds.

How to Welcome "A History of the World in 100 Objects"

In June of 2017, the Shanghai Museum hosted the exhibition "A History of the World in 100 Objects"—an exhibition so ambitious that it required 100 curators and four years of research into the extensive collection of the British Museum. The exhibition, which toured to a number of international destinations including Abu Dhabi, Tokyo, Canberra, and Beijing, would test Shanghai Museum's capacity for change. Outside the exhibition hall, through a series of podcasts coproduced with BBC4 and narrated by museum director Neil MacGregor, listeners, who hadn't even glimpsed the objects, were enthralled by stories about exquisite treasures told to them in a charming and down-to-earth manner.[1] The podcasts attracted a million listeners, prompting the museum to produce a book based on the same theme.

When the exhibition landed in Shanghai, it became an overnight success—in fact, it was one of the top ten thematic exhibitions in the world in terms of attendance according to the *Art Newspaper*.[2]

As the exhibition was free, which is not usually the situation for special traveling exhibitions, we saw record numbers of visitors, which pushed the museum to improve its procedures for dealing with crowds. On the day of the opening of the exhibition, visitors lined up outside the exhibition hall waiting in hot anticipation for a look at the objects on display. The next day we saw visitor numbers the likes of which are rarely seen at Shanghai Museum, and the figures would only increase as word of this unique exhibition spread through the city. The whole staff plunged into the task of managing the crowds, working on how to ensure a safer, more comfortable and satisfying experience for guests. Out of our brainstorming emerged a better approach to managing and receiving viewers, including iron railings, the installation of sunshades, revolving fans spraying cool mist, and on-the-spot medical care. In the interest of ensuring that visitors would avoid overly-long wait times, we capped visitor numbers at 8,000 for daytime visits. In addition, we placed notice boards to inform visitors of the average wait times. The museum worked with Shanghai TV's program "A Glimpse of the News" and launched the "queuing-up mate" campaign—which encouraged visitors to bring a friend to help pass the time, which could be as long as five to six hours. In the queuing area, we placed 20 portable displays on which Quick Response (QR) codes were printed. By

Figure 39 Crowds queue for the British Museum exhibition "A History of the World in 100 Objects" (2017), which was attended by 384,347 visitors.

scanning the code, "queue-ers" could read descriptions of what they would see in the exhibition hall. Fans traveling from cities as far away as Wenzhou, many university students, were quite keen to learn about the artifacts. One visitor from Hangzhou posted a guide to exhibition viewing that recommended external resources such as a BBC NHK documentary and other online sources for visitors who wanted to do their homework before the exhibition. In order to satisfy demand for the show, 29 nighttime slots were added, which included tours by museum staff and the regular opening hours were also extended. In total, the exhibition welcomed 384,347 viewers, which makes it the most popular exhibition in the museum's 65-year history.

From my perspective, this event provided a great real-life trial for us to test the limits of the free-admission policy. We used it to see how we might provide additional services to make each visit smooth and enjoyable—and memorable; the knowledge we gained will serve us well in the future.

Imported Exhibition, Local Products

As a way of helping to promote, support, and contextualize the exhibition for a local audience, the museum produced 180 new items of merchandise that, for those who could not make it to the exhibition, were available on the British Museum online store. When the store launched, on July

1, 2018, many of the items sold out within days.[3] This store, along with Shanghai Museum's successful store on the dominant e-commerce platform Taobao, featured an array of attractive souvenirs including hieroglyphic Scotch tape, stylish glass tumblers with gold cartoon pharaohs, and elegant fans with bamboo handles printed with Hosukai's signature "wave." During the exhibition period, we produced RMB 17 million in sales. In 2016, the Ministry of Culture issued a notice that encouraged museums to innovate and produce merchandise—more importantly, it stated that this revenue would go back into the museum budget either for designing new merchandise, improving visitor services, or as bonuses for staff. Our staff put in many unpaid overtime hours in order to allow the museum to remain open at night, not to mention the overtime put in before the opening of the exhibition. However, public museums do not have the culture of remunerating staff for overtime work; this needs to change in order to further the development of the museum sector.

But rather than focusing on the systematic problems of the museum sector, we sought to throw our weight behind the effort to build a "super connection" with our visitors, to create fulfilling experiences with the aim of rebranding our image. In my mind, a museum's commitment to the public and the experience of the public is a good yardstick of its overall success. This may not seem radical by today's standards, but given the situation of museums 30 years ago, and even today for some institutions, this represents a radical shift in attitude.

Making Objects Come Alive—
Creating Exhibition-Relevant Programming

On one level of programming, we focused on specialized topics and audiences, inviting renowned scholars such as Belinda Crerar, the exhibition planner in the British Museum, and Mu Tao and Yan Haiying, professors of history with Peking University. These free lectures covered topics such as the Age of Ramses II and the Age of Discovery.

On another level, we offered high-quality children's programming for different age groups. For example, we offered 9 courses, featuring 82 separate lessons, for kids from 6 to 9 and from 8 to 14. These courses include bilingual offerings such as "A Look at the History of the World"—a general history course—to "The Wondrous World of Shadow"—a course outlining the history of shadow puppetry. The programming even covered more lighthearted topics (something that is fairly unusual in China) such as "The History of Food for a Foodie." Many of these courses helped illuminate these 100 objects through various angles and entry points. The exhibition was also tied into other forms of programming, including two concerts themed "The Voice of 100 Objects—Concerts for Parents and Children at Shanghai Museum," and the "Museum Summer Camp," which involved specialized tours of the exhibition for families.

Finally, as part of the format of the exhibition, each museum chose to add a 101st object to the collection that had some deep meaning for both the museum and the history of humanity. Shanghai Museum picked the QR code as our representative object. Our motivations lay in the fact that the QR code connects people to knowledge, cultural objects to audiences, and is also an integral part of everyday life in China—used to buy groceries at the neighborhood wet market, used to exchange contacts with friends, and as a log-in method for most websites. By scanning the code, visitors also could add the WeChat social media channel of the Shanghai Museum, thus prolonging and extending their learning experience in a way similar to that of the BBC podcasts. Through this process, we gained 252,156 new followers. Given our hundreds of thousands of new followers, we thought the timing was right to roll out new services on our WeChat channel, including an in-app reservation system for night slots, educational programming, and an in-app exhibition guide, plus various other kinds of content related to the exhibition. Beyond our social media channels, we also received an overwhelming response from the press with 10,000 articles and features (including reprints) in most major media outlets. This response not only illustrates the public hunger for new kinds of exhibition content, but also provides a good example of how to properly "dock" a traveling show by providing not only adequate visitor services, but also new exhibition content, public programming, and even souvenirs that can help the public both understand the exhibition and bring these featured objects closer to home.

20

GUANGDONG MUSEUM

The Dawn of the Smart Museum

Wei Jun

In discussing the role of new museology in contemporary museum practice, scholar Davina DesRoches writes that rather than being "repositories of material culture that articulate personal and national identity," museums now engage in a "process of cultural exchange that perpetuates community dialogue and ongoing constructions of meaning."[1]

This is a radical change in the very definition of the museum. This new "post-museum" involves a recognition of the importance of "interpretation"—the voice we use to speak to the public—which signals a change in the power dynamic from the previous era, which privileged the voice of the curator above all else. The current dynamic involves a *conversation* between the visitor, the objects, and their personal life experience. This new stance, writes DesRoches, assumes that "welcoming of the visitor" has become "the museum's raison d'être."[2]

As a regional museum with a history of 59 years, Guangdong Museum certainly carries with it the weight of history, both its own and the global history of museums. But the museum, like other storied institutions in the West, is now embracing many of the tenets of new museology, placing a new importance on education, museum services, and outreach, while at the same time working to extend the reach and influence of the institution through digital means and improve its functionality through smart technologies. Part of this push is in the aim of expanding and exploring social spaces outside the walls of the museum—a concept we helped promote as early as 2004 in our adoption of the idea of "Museums without Borders." Museums without Borders emphasizes transnational and interdisciplinary exchanges and the sharing of resources,

information, and services both inside and outside the museum, thus breaking down barriers to development.

In particular, we believe that museums should be integrated with society, to walk with the public and to bring the functions of education, appreciation, and communication into different realms of public space. Part of this means taking the physical assets of the museum *literally* outside the museum walls to the corridors of the subway, the airports, malls, and parks and also communities, residential areas, retirement homes, and kindergartens. Many museums possess these aims but execute them haphazardly without extending this function through a systematic approach.

Guangdong Museum has played a proactive role in the expansion of the museum's space with our "Maritime Silk Road" initiative. This project falls under the umbrella of a government policy aimed at encouraging cooperation between Southern China, Southeast Asia, Oceania, and North Africa—the "One Belt, One Road" policy put forth by Xi Jinping.[3]

The "Maritime Silk Road" project involved a collaboration with Guangzhou Metro Company, which saw maritime-themed subway cars decorated floor to ceiling with colorful hand-drawn cartoon imagery, 3D installations where passengers could take selfies, and 57 cultural relics presented in display cases.

This project also included three tailor-made "culture trains," where subway riders had the chance to experience many of the functions of the museum on their daily commute. The exhibition saw a total of 2.94 million viewers over three

Figure 40 The Guangdong Museum (1959, 2004, Guangzhou), created by Rocco Design Architects, is modeled after an antique Chinese lacquer box. The museum became the showpiece of the Pearl River New Town district, located near the Guangzhou Opera House (2010, Zaha Hadid) within the Pearl River Green Belt. *Photography: Chao Zhen. Photo courtesy: Chinese Museums Association Architecture and Technology Committee, China Archive of Museum Architecture, and the Nanjing Museum*

Figure 41 Guangdong Museum brings the museum into the public space with "The Haitian Corridor," a Silk Road cultural hub, opened at the Baiyun Airport in Guangzhou on August 16, 2017. *Photo courtesy: Guangdong Museum*

months and resulted in two more "Museums in Subway" collaborations with the Guangzhou Metro Company.

The captive audience of these spaces attracts viewers who otherwise might not take the time to visit the museum. An airport is, in a sense, the perfect space for cultural experiences given the long periods spent waiting, with little in the way of entertainment. There are others examples of cooperation between museums and airports, including the Metropolitan Museum of Art (which has a store in the JFK Airport) and the Louvre (which has shown reproductions of works at CDG airport). These museums understand the importance of marketing in airports. But such collaborations often focus on the retail side and monetizing the IP resources of the museum. In 2017, we signed a cooperation agreement with Guangzhou Baiyun International Airport to jointly build a new brand based on the region of Guangdong through the sharing and promotion of cultural resources. The space consisted of 3,300 square meters in the Terminal 2 arrivals area, which featured a "Sky-Sea Corridor."

The theme of the "Sea" illustrates the 1,000-year history of Guangzhou Port, and the "Sky" was represented by aviation imagery. The corridor featured artifacts placed in glass vitrines that could be seen as either portholes or airplane windows. The corridor involved 3D displays and interactive educational activities. The first phase of the Sky-Sea Corridor exhibition lasted five months and welcomed 902,000 visitors. The success of this exhibition resulted in new cooperation for new museum experiences and exhibition spaces, bringing art, educational activities, and intangible cultural heritage to passengers. These experiences in the Guangzhou Subway and airport led us to explore other kinds of public spaces such as shopping malls, through exhibitions, arts, and interactive activities.

From Inward to Outward Focus

The social roles and responsibilities of museums are becoming an important part of museum practice and thinking. We firmly believe that a responsible museum should not only fulfill its own goals and responsibilities but also devote itself to promoting the development of museums in less-developed regions. In 2004, we began to build mobile museum networks that aimed to provide museum services and expertise to less sophisticated or poorly funded institutions. Over the past 14 years, we have continually optimized this service network and improved our modes of delivering these services.

The Regional Museums Co-Construction Plan and Resource Sharing Plan adopted by the museums of Guangdong Province uses a targeted approach to help ten small state or private museums each year to solve operations problems and provide technical counsel and staff training and resources, therefore gradually enabling a coordinated development strategy among the regional museums.

Our museum network thus evolved from a museum-oriented network to focusing on public welfare and creating a network without boundaries. This network now covers 114 museums of different types and numerous schools, villages, army facilities, and residential communities.

Second, we have moved from pure mobile (touring) exhibitions to comprehensive art and culture exhibitions. Apart from these touring exhibitions, we have introduced many other services to the public such as "mobile art and culture libraries," educational activities, professional skills training, and creative products. Third, we have moved from an attitude of passively waiting for visitors to proactively offering services to the public—for instance, making museums more accessible to disadvantaged groups including "left-behind children" (those raised solely by their grandparents in rural environments), lonely elderly residents, the physically challenged, and other marginalized groups. We take great pride in the fact that we extended access to our rich collection to residents all around Guangdong Province, with our 237 touring exhibitions attracting over 3.1 million visitors in 2017.

Some programs involved helping museums share their exhibition content with the public through the Digital Resources Access Plan, which made over 10,000 high-definition digital images of collection objects freely available to the public. Meanwhile, the Plan for Open Access to Materials has made our professional library accessible to the public. Researchers, scholars, and hobbyists can now, by appointment, access our collection of over 100,000 specialized and ancient books. Finally, we have reached unprecedented numbers of people, especially millennials, with our adoption of live streaming technology—one of the hottest trends in social media in China—providing exhibition tours, lectures, and educational programs. In the first three months of 2018, we reached over 900,000 people through our live stream.

Launching the Smart Museum

Around 2008, following IBM's launch of its "Smarter Planet, Smarter Cities" initiatives, which harnessed the power of the Internet of information technology, we began to see a whole new array of applications from smarter communities, to smart healthcare, to smart traffic management and smart travel. These innovations were changing both industry and the lifestyles of the average citizen.

These global trends are reflected in the government policy of "Internet+" which features interdisciplinary integration and innovation that is both human-centered and connected—a process that has the potential to disrupt different modes of service. Many believe that "intelligent" technology will be a distinctive feature of the museums of the future, which represents a revolution in the thinking and practice of museums as we know them today.[4]

Guangdong Museum was among the first batch of "Smart Museum" pioneers to apply technology to museums in China in 2014. For the past four years, we have devoted our time to improving the museum's capabilities in management, preservation, and services—to connect things (museums, collections, and equipment) and people (the public, museum audiences, and employees) through the Internet of Things, big data, cloud computing, artificial intelligence, and other network and communication technologies.

The Smart Museums Project focused on three aspects: smart preservation, smart management, and 3D smart preservation. When it came to the Smart Preservation System, we focused on building two systems, that is, a climate control monitoring system and a secure information management system. These two systems achieved real-time data monitoring of temperature, humidity, and pollutants (in spaces such as offices, storerooms, exhibition halls, and display cabinets), and realized other functions such as analyzing data, with sensors providing warning functions and automatic adjustments to maintain optimal conditions. For our Smart Management System, we built eight application systems that deal with collections management, digital resource management, and visitor information analysis. These applications helped us optimize our operations for information resource management, make scientifically informed decisions on projects, and standardize our operations management. Our smart service system employed intelligent systems to determine indoor positioning, VR and AR, intelligent navigation, and the inclusion of multimedia and new media elements to heighten visitor experience.

These examples of innovation represent a microcosm of the development of Chinese museums over the past ten years and the trend toward well-functioning, people-oriented, accessible institutions that help realize the goals of new museology in a Chinese context.

21

NATURAL HISTORY MUSEUMS

Underappreciated, Yet Wildly Popular

Jian Guan

In China, natural history museums have the power to attract large numbers of viewers. A stroll through the halls of the Shanghai Natural History Museum is like parting the Red Sea, for all the swells of children roving through the spacious exhibition halls. Even its now-dated older predecessor, the Shanghai Science and Technology Museum, sees six million visitors a year. Animals and dinosaurs, in particular, seem to possess a power to seduce viewers across all ages and educational backgrounds. Yet, surprisingly in Mainland China, only four natural history museums were built from 1949 to 1978, located in Beijing, Shanghai, Tianjin, and Dalian respectively.

Like other types of museums, natural history museums entered a period of rapid development in 1995. The natural history museums in Dalian, Tianjin, and Shanghai all witnessed the building of new, larger, and more sophisticated exhibition spaces at external sites, while the Beijing Museum of Natural History expanded within its original site. Beyond these expansions, large-scale natural history museums were built in five provincial capitals and municipalities directly under the central government, in the provinces of Jilin, Shaanxi, and Zhejiang.[1]

Specializations in Natural History

Over the past 40 years, geology museums as a category have seen the largest increase. Currently, there are over 100 museums in this category. This seemingly-random phenomenon can be attributed to the attention paid to the geosciences and science education by the government,

and it was also influenced by the government requirements for National Geological Parks—thus many parks built museums in the hopes of attaining this desirable designation. The Geological Museum of China in Beijing was renovated from its original site in 2003. Its exhibition space was restored to top-notch condition with a professional international exhibition design company that produced an Earth Exhibition Hall featuring a large globe across a whole floor of the museum.

By contrast, there has been a slow growth of planetariums. The Shanghai Planetarium is currently under construction as a branch of the Shanghai Science and Technology Museum. The sole large-scale professional planetarium in Mainland China is the 1957 Beijing Planetarium. In the early 21st century, this museum underwent an expansion and equipment upgrade on the original site. Hall B opened at the end of 2004—with a standard spherical panoramic screen, its 18-meter-wide cosmic theater was built to present films with magnificent stereoscopic effects and can accommodate 200 viewers.

The development of natural history museums has been marked by a dramatic increase in the professional standards of thematic museums and exhibition halls. Such museums include several dinosaur museums; perhaps most representative of these is the Zigong Dinosaur Museum, which opened in 1987. Dinosaur museums account for the largest proportion of these thematic natural history museums, largely due to new paleontological discoveries as well as a growing appetite from the public. Over the

Figure 42 Shanghai Natural History Museum (2015) is optimized for maximum visitor flow, while the latticed windows evoke the patterns of plant cell structures. Outside the glass wall, a multistory garden with numerous rockeries and pools as in a traditional Chinese garden. *Photography: Rebecca Catching*

past 30 years, dozens of thematic museums focusing on dinosaurs and fossils have been built, much to the delight of the public, especially the children.

Before 1978, many provincial-level natural history museums included collections and research departments as well as biological and paleontological galleries. Most provincial museums in China have been expanded to new sites, and thus the presentation of their specimen collections has been expanded and improved. The Yunnan Provincial Museum provides a fascinating example. During the construction of the new hall in 2008, one-quarter of the total exhibition area was allotted to display discoveries and research pertaining to the geology, biology, and prehistory of Yunnan. In order to solve the gaps in their collection, the museum embarked on in-depth exhibition planning and research in order to prepare for the exhibition hall design. The research demonstrated that the ethnic diversity of the province of Yunnan, which is home to more than 25 different ethnic minorities, was a result of the evolution of the natural environment. The terrain of

the mountainous province created pockets of human habitation that are connected by rivers, which helped nourish these unique settlements.

In line with the policy of having governments at all levels to provide support for Chinese museums, the Chinese Academy of Sciences issued policies to encourage research institutes to actively establish natural history museums. The Chinese Vertebrate Paleontology Museum was opened in 1995, located on the first floor of the newly built Institute of Vertebrate Paleontology and Paleoanthropology of the Chinese Academy of Sciences. It was the first museum established and managed directly by the Chinese Academy of Sciences. Later, the Nanjing Paleontology Museum and Kunming Animal Museum were opened to the public in 2004 and 2006, respectively. Currently, there is also the National Animal Museum (Beijing), the Shanghai Insect Museum, and the Museum of Aquatic Organisms in Wuhan. These institute-built museums have not only expanded the range of nature museums but have also become a force for popularizing cultivating scientific literacy.

Figure 43 The façade of Yunnan Museum (2015, Guandu District) was inspired by the region's stone forests—craggy karst formations that jut out from the landscape. Conceived as both stone structures and stacked boxes containing the museum's treasures. *Photography: Chao Zhen. Photo courtesy: Chinese Museums Association Architecture and Technology Committee, China Archive of Museum Architecture, and the Nanjing Museum*

Compared with historical and archaeological museums, China's natural history museums have maintained closer contact with the global museum communities, partially because it is a requirement for their profession. For example, taxonomic studies, which focus on the naming of species, must be compared with the existing species and taxonomies elsewhere.

Several of the large, comprehensive natural history museums very quickly increased their communication with foreign museums through introductions, learning, and exchange, following the Reform and Opening-Up. For example, in 1981, the Beijing Museum of Natural History sent letters to foreign natural history museums, with a proposal that they exchange their academic journals, thus beginning a 40-year history of academic exchange with museums and research institutes. In 1978, the Australian Wildlife Exhibition was exhibited at the Beijing Museum of Natural History as a cultural exchange between the two countries. One of the earliest foreign exhibitions in Mainland China, it not only attracted a long queue of Beijing citizens but also broadened the horizons of the museum profession as a whole.

The Beijing Museum of Natural History has also toured its dinosaur collections in Asia and North America with great success while introducing foreign exhibitions to their own viewers. The fees earned by these touring shows have indeed helped to cover the gaps in operational funding, but more importantly, the professionals and managers participating in the tours have gained precious opportunities to gain firsthand insights of how to better expand the scientific content and aesthetic design of exhibitions.

In 1992, after seeking a partial sponsorship from the China-Britain Science and Culture Association, the Beijing Museum of Natural History invited the deputy director of the Public Service Department of London's Museum of Natural History to give lectures in seven Chinese cities, explaining the concepts and methods of his museum, which became a globally emulated method. This "New Exhibition Scheme" involved images and films displayed in an immersive layout and privileged experiential learning, positioning the museum as a place of leisure in which the public can freely roam, as in a park or shopping center. Therefore, natural history museums needed to have a deep understanding of their viewers through conducting market research and attracting the public by means of a series of subversive reforms such as exhibition planning that involved new ways of building design teams, and a sharp adjustment in the discourse power. At that time, many museums were troubled, as they barely had enough money to fix basic problems such as leaky roofs. But this three-week lecture series did much for the community's understanding of the nature, mission, and advanced methods of contemporary museums.

The economic growth brought about by China's Reform and Opening-Up has also allowed for more funds for collections and research. Thus, the Beijing Museum of Natural History was able to collect specimens in the Paracel Islands and the surrounding seas as well as to participate in scientific expeditions and specimen collection on the Qinghai-Tibet Plateau and the Tianshan Mountains. This new funding brought about a significant increase in the number of specimens and fossils of various professional categories, including many valuable types of specimens.

The new collections have also enhanced the collaborative research of the Beijing Museum of Natural History with its foreign counterparts. For instance, the fossils of 15 million years ago were discovered in Tongxin, Ningxia. Through collaborative research with the world's leading ancient anthropologists, the specimens were restored to the best possible condition. In addition, the museum published papers in the world's most authoritative anthropological journals, thus expanding its reputation around the globe. Moreover, the museum also presented these new collections and their excellent research achievements to the public through exhibitions. In 1997, new collections of 16 complete skeletons, including the world's first complete skeleton-like fossil, were exhibited in a large-scale landscape in this museum's thematic exhibition, "The Long Nose in History." These specimens were exhibited outside the case and told vivid stories about the animals and the environment, setting a precedent for interactive exhibitions in natural history museums.

This process has not been easy, characterized by the clash of ideas and constant changes in terms of the fundamental philosophy of exhibition making. The Beijing Museum of Natural History engaged in these debates in 1988, when they redesigned their exhibits on human evolution. In the early phase of China's Reform and Opening-Up, this basic exhibition was revised and titled "The Origin of Man," consisting of three units: "Man as a Unique Animal," "The Origin of Man," and "The Development of the Individual." This redesign provoked a number of heated discussions such as:

> Is it possible to avoid Engels's view that the act of *labor* is what defines man from other animals? Is it possible to use the concept of the "Middle Stone Age"—a concept that had yet to appear in Chinese textbooks? And finally, is it possible to present content related to sex in the exhibition? After intense debate with extensive media participation, the exhibition was displayed without any modifications. This element of critical debate set a benchmark for how other institutions could proceed.

After 30 years of reform, China's natural history museums have matured to the point where they can combine innovations from overseas with resources and vision that

Jian Guan

are unique to China. Take, for instance, the new Shanghai Museum of Natural History, opened in 2014 under the theme of "Nature, Humanity, and Harmony." Through three themes, "The Concerto of Evolution," "The Scroll Painting of Life," and "The Epic of Civilization," the Shanghai Museum of Natural History presented ten subthemes, including "The Mystery of Our Origins," "The River of Life," "Shades of Life," "Tied to the Earth," "The Shanghai Story," and "The Road to the Future." Both local and international visitors were impressed by the exhibits, participated in experiential activities, and enjoyed demonstrations that are on par with those of world-class nature museums.

Since the 1980s, private collectors have shared their collections through museums or exhibition halls. For example, the Chen Baocai Butterfly Museum in Shanghai, with a meager space of only 20 square meters (the size of a room in a Shanghai apartment), manages to display more than 600 kinds of domestic and 200 foreign butterfly specimens, which were collected by the dedicated Mr. Chen. As one of the earliest private natural history museums in China, this butterfly museum evoked a warm response from citizens and the greater museum industry.

Non-state-owned natural history museums or exhibition halls, often characterized by their small size, specific themes, and unique character, attract viewers with their quirkiness and play a vital role in this sector. The earlier nature museums and showrooms are mostly themed around dinosaur-based fossils, rare stones (rocks and minerals with strong ornamental value), petrified wood, and insects. The quantity and size of non-state-owned nature museums are growing tremendously along with the reforms, increased disposable income, and the public's growing demands for a more diversified cultural life and education.

As shopping malls struggle with the effects of the e-commerce boom, more and more turn to museums to open up in high-end retail complexes. Since 2017, China Resource (Holdings) Co., Ltd., has opened a specialized exhibition center in its MIXC Shopping Center in several cities. "Time-Traveling through Existence" was first exhibited at the Chengdu MIXC Exhibition Center in June 2017. This 800-square-meter exhibition traversed various geological eras continuing into the future, explaining the shared destiny of humans and the environment and presenting strong messages of environmental protection.

In 2018, the Grandview Plaza in Guangzhou, with an area of 300,000 square meters, one of the largest shopping centers in Asia, opened China's first large-scale marine biology museum in a shopping center, the Grandview Nature Museum. It is a comprehensive nature museum featuring groundbreaking collections on astronomy, geology, biology, and human collections.

Despite its location in a mall, the Grandview Nature Museum is built to the standards of comprehensive nature museums, but it is different from public, private, or business models in several ways. First, it has a large number of high-quality and world-class collections that required considerable investment. Second, through a lot of dioramas, with in-depth interpretations and interactive exhibitions, the story of the evolution of life is illustrated through science, art, and new media. For example, one-third of the nature exploration center is dedicated to children, while the "Future Nature" high-tech exhibition is mainly targeted toward youth (the main demographic of the shopping center). The 3,000-square-meter space received nearly 10,000 visitors within the first two days of its opening.

Since 2005, the American collector Mr. Kenneth E. Behring has donated large numbers of specimens and mounts to dozens of museums in China. Originating from Africa, America, Europe, and Australia, these are well-made specimens of high scientific and aesthetic value. The exhibits featuring Mr. Behring's donations involve creating large-scale landscapes, where the animals walk out from their "natural habitat," enabling the Chinese public to see the wild animals from every continent in their "ecological context."

Though Chinese museums have made great strides in the past 40 years, the problem of supply remains, as public demand for museums outstrips the number of institutions. The museum sector is now beginning to rethink *how* and *where* culture is supplied to better enable convenient access to museums for Chinese urban and rural residents and to instill in them a sense of compassion toward the natural world. Harnessing the popularity of natural history museums with the general public, we can hope to bring about a deeper understanding of our current geological epoch—the Anthropocene—an era characterized by momentous environmental changes incurred by the frenzied activities of humankind.

22

SUZHOU MUSEUM

Harnessing the Power of People, Products, and Place

Chen Ruijin

A Confluence of Tradition and Cosmopolitan

On July 4, 2008, the *New York Times* ran an article on the front page written by art critic Holland Cotter, who claimed that "The new city museum in Suzhou is a Modernist showcase par excellence, pitched to international consumption . . . its clean lines and cream-and-gray architecture would look equally at home in Paris or New York. So would the Spartan galleries, which exude art-speaks-for-itself Western taste and are as suited to party giving as art viewing."[1]

Cotter's words very much capture I. M. Pei's reinterpretation of classical Suzhou architecture, but they speak as well to the spirit of the museum itself—which seeks to give contemporary expressions to ancient things. Like a piece of double-sided embroidery that features a different design on each side of the cloth, Pei's design possesses both traditional and contemporary charms, reaching different people in different ways.

Pei himself was born in Suzhou and has a family history in the region dating back 600 years; thus, it is fitting that his design feeds back into the traditional nature of the area with nods to the architectural vernacular (white walls, gray accents, and gray roof) in a modern adaptation of a *siheyuan* courtyard house. At the same time, we mustn't forget that it was designed by an architect described as the "senior statesman of modernism." It differs from traditional Suzhou architecture in its use of different materials (slate tiles instead of clay) and in its spatial progression and use of natural light and shadow, which articulates the interior of the museum in a way that is not normally observed in the dark interiors of traditional Suzhou-style homes.

This light, airy nature and his use of geometric shapes and angular lines—standing in contrast to the sinuous shapes found in Suzhou gardens—brings a cosmopolitan presence to the ancient quarter, placing Suzhou's rich culture in a more international context. The area in the northeast side of the city is the home to elaborately choreographed gardens, with dancing paths, swaying banana leaves, and bonsais holding mysterious poses. A treasure of architectural and horticultural beauty, the quarter is home to Zhongwang Palace, the Garden of the Humble Administrator, and the Lion Forest Garden. Beyond gardens, there are also other cultural institutions such as the Suzhou Arts and Crafts Museum (a national folk museum dedicated to local craftsmanship), the Kun Opera (a key element of intangible heritage), and the Suzhou Opera Museum, featuring *pingtan* (a form of storytelling in Suzhou dialect, involving arias and stringed instruments).

Unlike many other urban museums that seek to make a grand and dominating statement focusing on spectacle, the museum seems to blend elegantly into the surrounding areas like a modern continuation of the Humble Administrator's garden. Without too much ornamentation or flamboyant gestures, it creates an amicable dialogue with the other buildings in the quarter, like two *pingtan* performers bantering on stage.

Speaking to Place and the Legacy of Regional Civilizations

As a major cultural venue in the city, the museum is not only a recorder or preserver of historical culture, but also bears the responsibility to promote and develop culture within the urban context. When visitors go to an unfamiliar city, they develop a habit of visiting the city museum first, because a museum allows them to quickly understand the city's history, and culture.

When you visit the Capital Museum in Beijing, you can have a taste of the ancient capital of Beijing and learn about Beijing folk customs. When you visit the Hunan Museum, you are able to experience the past and present of Hunan; when you visit the Shanxi Museum in Taiyuan, you will become acquainted with the story of Shanxi merchants; and when you visit the Guangdong Museum, you can immerse yourself in Lingnan culture—the cultural legacy of Southern China. The differences between one city and another, between one museum and another, become obvious as we stroll through the exhibition halls.

For example, Suzhou, a historical and cultural city, has a history of more than 10,000 years, including over 5,000 years of civilization, and was established as a city 2,500 years ago. The ethos of *shangwu* (warrior worship) shared by Wuyue people—a prominent cultural group in the Yangtze River Delta during the Spring and Autumn Period

(770–476 BC)—gradually faded; it was replaced by *chongwen*, the adoration of text and literature. It became the new symbol of Suzhou when Fan Zhongyan, a famous official in the Northern Song dynasty (960–1127), breathed life into Suzhou's floundering system of prefectural schools.

The Suzhou Museum takes on the important mission of preserving, spreading, and promoting culture and art to the public. By adhering to its own social mission, the Suzhou Museum has actively organized various thematic exhibitions that focus on local cultures in addition to a series of foundational exhibitions—branded by the character *Wu* 吴 (as in the Wuyue people) to reflect the indigenous nature of the museum's mission.

In 2012, the Suzhou Museum launched a series of exhibitions under the "Wu" umbrella, titled "Wu Men Si Jia" ("The Four Masters of the Ming Dynasty"), which explored the accelerating handicraft industry, the increasingly prosperous nature of urban life, and the thriving *literati* class[2] in Ming-dynasty Suzhou. As the positioning fit well into local culture, the exhibition achieved a good response, not only attracting attention from museum professionals, but also evoking the passionate participa-

Figure 44 The Suzhou Museum (1960, 2006), designed by I. M. Pei, reflects the spirit of the Southern literati scholar garden with its focus on mountains and water, yet employs a more modern geometric aesthetic. *Photography: Zhangzhugang*

tion of the local citizens. This exhibition was deemed the must-see show of the year. In 2016, the Suzhou Museum planned another elaborate exhibition, "Suzhou Collectors in the Qing Dynasty," which displayed the quintessential collections from several historically important Suzhou families, speaking to the *literati* aesthetic and the culture of Suzhou in the Qing dynasty.

Creating a Community to Reinforce the Mission

All exhibitions very much speak to the place of Suzhou, harnessing the civic pride of the city and the culture to provoke deeper learning and appreciation of these lost arts and historical personalities. By choosing different classical subjects to appeal to different demographics, we try to find ways to bring classical culture to a broad range of groups. Events such as our "Impression @ Su Bo" painting contests solicited artwork from primary school students, asking them to draw us their "museum of the future." Meanwhile our "Knowledge and Culture Forum" is more focused on theoretical learning and involves lectures on the differences between Chinese and Western styles of painting.

Tapping into both the figurative and literal notions of outreach, our "Touching Culture" program allows blind visitors to experience artifacts in a tactile manner. Family activities allow children to use their hands, engaging in structured creativity by learning to make Ming dynasty hair accessories. Yet we also invite visitors to occasionally "leave the kids at home." For instance, on Valentine's Day, we held an event aimed primarily at couples, which used the love story of painter Wu Hufan and his wife, Pan Jingshu, as a starting point for an activity that included a lecture on painting appreciation, combined with a traditional painting demonstration and a chance for guests to try their hand at re-creating Wu's delicate brushstrokes.

Outreach has not typically been a major focus of Chinese museums, but gradually they are beginning to make it more of a priority. In addition to our work with the visually impaired community, we have also created traveling exhibitions composed of mobile exhibition panels, which we have sent out into 40 different communities around Suzhou, including elementary schools, businesses, schools for the hearing impaired, seniors' homes, orphanages, and communities of new immigrants to Suzhou. Our "Wenbo Courses" have also been held in children's community centers in rural areas. This included the development of 25 highly readable courses focusing on the architecture of I. M. Pei, blue-and-white porcelain design, an introduction to the symbolic carvings found on traditional jade pendants, and finally the history of Suzhou pastries and sweets. All of these are closely integrated to the characteristics of Suzhou culture and museums. Furthermore, we have compiled this traditional knowledge in textbook form in *Understanding Suzhou: A Course on Tradition from the Suzhou Museum*.

Creating Deeper Connections through Volunteers

While China has a volunteering ethos that dates back to Confucian and Taoist thinkers, a native tradition that was reiterated and reinforced after 1949, the practice of volunteering in museums began only a decade ago. In this short time, the Suzhou Museum has made great strides and received national recognition.

We currently engage 163 volunteers who provide 10,316 hours of service per year, helping to supplement certain functions of the museum where we were short-staffed, acting as guides and interpreters. One of their key functions was helping with crowd control—given the newness of the museum experience, many visitors are not aware of museum etiquette. Following the example of the Palace Museum Taipei, we engaged volunteers to provide education and guidance, holding up signs to remind visitors of restrictions on flash photography and to keep their voices down—these efforts helped to maintain a quality visiting experience for all guests.

The volunteers provide vital services to the museum, but we also take great pains to give back in the form of providing social and educational opportunities. After the opening of the museum, we created 12 senior volunteer posts to provide guidance and counseling on our public programming. These senior volunteers not only helped us solve some of our staffing problems but also enthusiastically participated in our discussions, providing many creative suggestions.

The museum provides a variety of benefits; for instance, we regularly organize experts to give lectures on topics such as the local history of Suzhou, bronze casting techniques, ceramics, and jade identification techniques. These activities have the dual function of boosting volunteer morale and improving their interpretative skills. We even try to create a bit of a competitive spirit with our "Learning in Suzhou Museum" quiz contest. Each year our most exceptional volunteers are recognized through our "Top Volunteer Awards Ceremony," the winners of which will go on to be recognized at a national level.

The volunteer program is not merely confined to the Suzhou Museum. We organize cycling and hiking trips and connect with other volunteering groups in the region to offer opportunities for different kinds of volunteering experiences, such as caring for the marginalized and disadvantaged. Volunteers also receive free organized trips to other museums in China, and we frequently share with these museums on a cross-institutional basis to learn about best practices in the industry.

Besides providing valuable experience for Chinese youth to build confidence and leadership skills, the volunteers visitor's contribute to the experience of the museum. One of our visitors remarked, "The most impressive part of my visit to Suzhou Museum was its volunteer service, and its efforts to create a genuine space for citizens." After his visit on May 11, 2008, Holland Cotter lauded the program, remarking on "the surprising number of excellent English-speaking volunteers who are nowhere to be found in many other museums around China."

Digital Apps as Virtual Docents

Along with our active social media presence on platforms such as Weibo (Chinese Twitter) and WeChat (a multifunctional social media platform), we launched the AR-Museum app, which has injected new learning opportunities into the visitor experience. The app not only aids in navigation but also uses AR technology to create different kinds of animations (for instance, smoke emerging from an incense holder), which help explain the function of the various objects. Pop-up videos of museum staff help to explain the various stories behind the architecture and artifacts. Three-dimensional scans, close-up images of artifacts, and zoom capabilities allow for visitors to get a closer look at the objects behind the glass. The app includes both additional text and audio-guide capabilities provided in a number of regional dialects.

Public Engagement through Merchandise

Museum merchandise, derivatives, and IP have been a hot topic in museum circles in recent years due to official directives from the government in 2016 that encouraged rapid development of infrastructure for a range of cultural products (for more on this see chapter 20). Under the direction of the Ministry of Culture, 92 museums became the first batch of institutions participating in a nationwide project to connect products to their collections.

Some museums are already at the forefront, such as Shanghai Museum and the Palace Museum, with large, impressive product ranges. Many museums are also taking advantage of China's e-commerce wave, using platforms such as Taobao—China's answer to Amazon—to reach out to nonvisitors through the power of online shopping.

The National Museum of China has linked up with Alibaba Group—another major e-commerce and IT company—and built an online trading platform called Cultural Innovation China.[3] The museum provided access to the intellectual property of 400 items for use as part of the cooperation and has already launched their "offline operations center" located in the Shanghai Waigaoqiao Free Trade Zone. The goal of the center is to provide a variety of services related to creative industries and connect resources, such as documents, scanned images, and other IPs with the needs of the private sector. Meanwhile, the Palace Museum has established a long-term partnership with Tencent, another IT and e-commerce firm, and opened a series of classic IPs to be employed in various fields such as social platforms, games, animation, literature, and talent training. A series of 10 apps, which are part of the collaboration, can now be found on app stores (see chapter 18 for details).

In June 2016, the Suzhou Museum launched its own cooperation with the Taobao store by uniting three clothing brands. Working with these brands, they created a series of 24 designs with 11 items put into mass production. The inspiration for the designs was derived from the museum's unique architecture and its collection under the theme of "walking history." The products include everything from trendy jackets featuring stylized outlines of mountain landscapes rendered in sequins and pinstripes, to pendants echoing the shapes of Suzhou garden windows, to long, flowing cosplay gowns with delicate patterns of coy, in the style of Chinese painting. The Suzhou Museum also has an existing online store with unique gifts such as cups in the shape of Chinese chops (seals), and the Creative Landscape Project, which uses mountains as a motif in products such as stainless steel rulers and bamboo mobile phone holders. Suzhou Museum also has its own mascot, a cartoon character named Tang Yin, who shares the same name as the most famous artist, calligrapher, and poet of the Ming dynasty. The museum licensed the character to Nestlé, which produced a set of teas using Tang Yin as the paper tag at the end of the tea bag. Tang Yin's arms drape over the lip of the cup, so solving that age-old design flaw where the tag falls into the tea. The online store even features cute promotional videos to explain how these products can be used. This Nestlé cooperation not only resulted in an interesting product but earned the museum 140,000 RMB over three months in licensing fees.

The creation of these products also involved an element of public participation via crowdfunding. In 2017, our products were officially launched on the Taobao crowdfunding platform, attracting the participation of 708 people who contributed another 140,000 yuan, which was more than double our target. This new method of crowdfunding not only helped us tap into funding from our social network but also helped us collect opinions from visitors to develop products with a broad public appeal. In this way, the audience could participate in an impactful manner in both the construction of the museum and the promotion and appreciation of traditional culture. Like the visitors who bought the Tang Yin tea, they can have culture infused into their everyday lives in a way that is both meaningful *and*, most importantly, fun.

23

JINGDEZHEN IMPERIAL KILN MUSEUM

Embers of Memory

Zhu Pei

The Jingdezhen Imperial Kiln Museum is in the historic center of Jingdezhen. This was once a key site of porcelain-making in China, and thus it is no surprise that nearby we find a number of historic Ming and Qing dynasty kilns of various sizes scattered around the area. In creating this museum, we had to not only dialogue with this site specificity but also convey the history of porcelain in China and the kiln in the context of place-making and in the creation of a sense of community.

The city of Jingdezhen was forged through its kilns and became prosperous through its porcelain. Brick kilns not only originated in Jingdezhen, but they also provided sustenance to its people and functioned as a stage for civil society—for the performance of the ritual of everyday activities and communication between Jingdezhen's residents. Centuries ago, on cold winter mornings, children would walk by the kilns and pick up a brick on their way to school—grasping these bricks close to their chests in order to stave off the cold. In the summer, when the kilns were not in use, the children were drawn in by the cool, moist air coming from inside the kilns. Young people would gather there to chat, and old people would often meet there to while away the time.

The Imperial Kiln Museum is inspired by the embers of memory that still flicker within these dilapidated sites—and the architecture itself attempts to keep these memories warm. The kiln is characterized by a particular oriental-style arch, and there is a unique "temporal" and "thermal" connection to memory of the kiln bricks—the form they create (the kiln itself), the porcelain they produce, and the blood and the livelihood of the Jingdezhen people.

It's not only that the form of the kiln melds into the history of the city; it's also that the bricks that are used to construct the kiln can be felt and understood by the citizens in an intimate way. When the bricks reach a certain point in their life cycle, their ability to hold heat diminishes and they are "retired" to become bricks used for building local houses. Given that early on, Jingdezhen's kilns had become an important part of the life of the city and its memories, there was an inherent logic in choosing the form of the kiln as one of our architectural motifs.

In the site plan, arched kiln forms of various volumes and sizes are laid out in a random way like fallen trees. Some are closer; some are further apart, but like a forest, the space has a relaxed and natural atmosphere. Visitors wandering through the brick arches will experience the reciprocal effects of theory and practice—an architectural space that is familiar and unfamiliar at the same time.

The building is divided into an above-ground level and a below-ground level. The entrance and lobby are placed on the ground level in such a way that when the visitor approaches the museum, they can immediately feel intimately connected with the dimensions of the space. At the same time, the scale is such that the site maintains a similarity with the other buildings in the city, thus solidifying the connection between the kilns and Jingdezhen, between Jingdezhen and the kilns. More important is that this experience of entering the building is also very similar to that of the craftsmen—the visitor is literally walking in the footsteps of the porcelain masters who would enter the kilns to place wares to be fired.

Figure 45 Zhu Pei's design for the Jingdezhen Imperial Kiln Museum explores how ancient kilns became social destinations for the local community; they were warm in the winter and cool in the summer, which gave residents many reasons to congregate in and around the kilns. *Courtesy: Studio Zhu Pei*

Figure 46 Zhu Pei's sketch of the Jingdezhen Imperial Kiln Museum (2017) shows its harmonious placement within the landscape, which reflects the forms of the surrounding hills. *Photo courtesy: Studio Zhu Pei*

Walking in through the tranquil space on the surface level, strolling through the lobby and turning to the left, the viewer slowly enters a series of experiential exhibition spaces that vary slightly in size and alternate between inside and outside spaces. Traversing through the deep history provided by these historical relics and ancient sunken courtyards, the viewer is initiated into a voyage of kilns, porcelain, and humankind. From the lobby turning right, viewers see a bookstore, café, coffee shop, teahouse, and ultimately end their journey in the semi-outdoor space below the arches, stooping to observe the glinting light on the rough surface of the arch as the sun reflects off the ripples in the water. The low placement of the seams on the horizon lures visitors into taking a seat on the ground. The lengthening horizontal lines on the earth's surface created by the imperial kiln create an eye-catching sight—an unexpected surprise set up for the viewer to stumble upon. Before the viewers have entered the lobby, as they walk in the direction of the auditorium, passing through a vertical cut-out seam, they have the unique experience of seeing the Linglong pavilion through the window created by the seam—a sight that is at once surprising and familiar.

Inside the museum, the permanent exhibitions are located in closed loop on one level, with two temporary exhibition halls to be used as needed. They can be separately incorporated into the loop—into the exhibition as a whole—or exist independently because they have independent entrances. Another interesting feature of the museum is the incorporation of the process of ancient porcelain restoration, which becomes an important part of the exhibition narrative.

The office building, located on the extreme north part of a relatively independent arch-building placed on a southeast axis with its own entrance, is peaceful and hidden. Trucks can be backed up into the south end of the arch in a closed space within the arch to safely offload goods.

CONCLUSION

Toward a Sustainable Future: "Feeling the Stones as We Cross the River"

Javier Jimenez, Gail Lord, and Rebecca Catching

If museum development followed a logic similar to the market economy, wherein a "boom" is likely to be followed by a "bust," forecasters would be predicting a downturn in the museum growth cycle sometime soon. But the forecasters would be missing something: museum values are deeply embedded in society, and a downturn is more likely to be a period of consolidation than a "bust." Nonetheless, sustainability is a concern for all museums in all places. In this conclusion, we look into the future of museums in China and other countries where we can expect rapid development, and at museums in the global north and west that are perhaps already in a period of consolidation.

The way museums are growing in China reinforces how people think of China, which can be synthesized as "fast" and "big." Indeed, China is the country with the most megacities[1] in the world: 15 out of 47 as of 2017. A small city in China is likely to be larger than most metropolises in Europe. The same principle tends to apply to museums: most of the new museums that China has built in the last 20 years are larger than their counterparts elsewhere. A 10,000-square-meter facility in China is medium to small, whereas in the West it would be considered large. If cities are bigger, to some extent, it is natural to think that museums should also be bigger. However, while some of the earlier urban development models in China, based on scale and rapid growth, are being reassessed through a more human and environmentally friendly lens, with focus on place-making and gathering spaces, a similar shift is taking place with museums. Future plans call for more moderate-size museums.

The issue of rightsizing museums is also being discussed in the West. The Verbier Art Summit of 2017, organized in partnership with the Stedelijk Museum Amsterdam, addressed the rare topic of degrowth in museums: *Size Matters! (De)Growth of the 21st Century Art Museum.* Among the key conclusions from the summit were that "A palpable degree of 'gigantomania' has mirrored the processes of globalization since the 1990s" and museums have enthusiastically engaged in the process, and "The thinking and approaches of the allied art institutions . . . to growth has been largely one-dimensional and centered on size."[2]

We can summarize the many sustainability challenges discussed in the preceding 23 chapters as these five:

- lack of planning,

- prioritizing container over content,

- misunderstanding the reality of museum operating costs and earned revenues,

- overreliance on one source of funding, and

- underestimating the importance of creativity and innovation within the museum.

These challenges are not exclusive to China. On the contrary, they are well proven in the majority of museum ecosystems worldwide. Future sustainability depends on museums implementing remedial actions to turn these challenges into opportunities.

The museum boom has led to many badly planned museums all around the world. It is not sufficiently understood that museums rank among the more complex building types alongside airports and hospitals. Museums are often envisioned and designed by aspiring architects without sufficient reflection and consideration of the needs of the collections, future occupants, and audiences.[3] To properly assess museum needs requires a process of consensus-building with multiple stakeholders, as well as the alignment of very different disciplines and sensitivities, including architects, educators, artists, politicians, community organizations, and academics. A museum that does not meet international museum standards with respect to professional staff, climate control, and safety and security, for example, will not be taken seriously by peers and will not be able to borrow exhibitions that are so much in demand. Correcting this lack of planning late in the process is so expensive that more often than not institutions decide to live with them.

Inspiring and symbolic museum architecture is important for place-making, city branding, tourism, and community pride. However, the balance between container and content is key. And the overhead costs of extravagant architecture and lack of collections have been devastating for some new museums. The owner, whether a government, a civil society institution, or a developer, may commission an architectural icon, but managing the museum to deliver meaningful content and be a public gathering space and an engine of knowledge requires more than an inspiring building. It requires a clear and powerful vision, a capable leader, and a highly qualified team with specific skills and the ability to work across departments to benefit the visitor and the creation of new knowledge. These are goals for which there is no shortcut. Here is where growing professionalism among museum workers is key to sustainability. The opportunity to travel, to participate in international discourse, webinars, and courses, cannot be underestimated. The Chinese philosophy of "opening up to the world" has been instrumental to positive museum growth.

As urban densification and real estate booms have become dominant features of 21st-century cities worldwide, museums in China and elsewhere are increasingly created by city economic development departments and real estate developers who assume that museums are like commercial tenants that have profit as an attainable goal. Museums, however, have different goals, and they are staff-intensive operations that need to be maintained to high standards and filled with changing content to engage visitors. The numbers who attend museums may be higher than for a retail tenant, but they are more costly to operate. From the revenue side, "mission-driven" museums cannot charge visitors the actual cost of programs, preservation, and exhibitions, because if they did, they would be so expensive that their educational mission would be in question. In China most museums offer free admission, which has resulted in an enthusiastic and growing attendance that can benefit commercial neighbors. But whether charging or noncharging, a financial gap between revenues and expenses is to be expected, and this gap needs to be covered with external funding from private or public sources as well as the museum's earned revenues from rentals and retail (assuming space and staff for these functions has been planned). Unfortunately, in boom times most museum promoters ignore these realities and make the decision to build a museum if they can afford the short-term construction costs, without bearing in mind that the annual operating subsidy will frequently equal the total capital investment approximately every seven years for years to come.

Funding for museums varies by region and by political priorities everywhere in the world, including China. While China continues to invest in museum operations, this could change. In Europe, for example, where high levels of cultural funding were once the norm, the financial crisis that started in 2007 was the definitive blow in a succession of public funding cuts that forced a change of mentality by museum managers toward greater cooperation with the private sector, new commercial and entertainment offerings, and creative revenue strategies. The Prado Museum in Madrid saw its public funding decrease from 86 percent of its total budget in 2003 to 37 percent in just a decade. By completely changing its mentality and even its governance model it managed to cover the gap with private funding and even increase its total budget while doing so. In the United Kingdom, the Museums Association conducted a survey[4] to assess the extent and impact of public funding cuts between 2009 and 2013 and found out that there had been a 25 percent average reduction in public funding during the period, and that 49 percent of museums had experienced a cut in the last year alone (2013). The consequences included (for 2013 alone): closure of whole or parts of sites (29 percent), cuts in staff (37 percent), reduction in programs and temporary exhibitions (23 percent), and on the brighter side consolidation of new governance and funding schemes and more self-generated income (42 percent). Luckily, the museum sector is a resilient one, and as public funding decreases, a new private network of friends, donors, patrons, and members may take its place and support in a sustained manner. China is in the process of encouraging such independent museum support, the creation of museum governing and advisory boards, and developing the requisite incentives.

Javier Jimenez, Gail Lord, and Rebecca Catching

As we have seen, museum funding in China is very complex, and a transition is taking place in legislation that allows many museums to reinvest earned revenues (from merchandise, rentals, and programs) into museum operations. European museums only made this change 20 to 30 years ago. The United States developed a successful plural funding model from its earliest museums. Meanwhile, countries like India and Egypt, which are most likely to experience the next museum building boom, do not have the legal framework for museums to be supported by a mixed economy of private, public, and earned revenues—plural funding. Now is the time to put in place legislative systems and incentives so that museums can benefit from plural funding without the risk of domination by any one funder.

Chinese museums are more open than many of their Western counterparts to embrace innovation and creativity. Over the years, Chinese museums have demonstrated an impressive capacity to respond to changes in demographics, public interest, new technologies, and government policies, as reflected in the chapters of this book. Overcoming the negative images of museums of the past and continuing their transformation into places of relevance as well as scholarship is a key factor in sustainability.

This book has been a journey into the most rapidly growing museum sector in the world. As editors, we have had the benefit of experts recommended by the Chinese Museums Association as well as Western authors who have spent decades working with Chinese museums. It surprised us how many of the successes and challenges of Chinese museums correspond to Western experience, such as the success of digital technology, love of storytelling, the attraction of iconic architecture, and the professionalization of the sector. The challenges enumerated above had a familiar ring. In China all the successes and challenges are on a larger scale than we could have imagined, despite our considerable experience working with Chinese colleagues. Museums with their core functions of collection, preservation, education, creation of new knowledge, and social engagement are both profoundly local and brilliantly global, especially in the realm of exhibitions and the exercise of cultural diplomacy and soft power. Whether in a boom phase as in China or consolidation as in the West, museums always learn from each other. As for meeting the great challenge of future sustainability, it likely will be a combination of creativity, long-term planning, and "feeling the stones as we cross the river."

NOTES

Introduction

1. See Duan Yong, chapter 3 of this book.

2. Guido Guerzoni, "The Museum Building Boom," in *Cities, Museums and Soft Power*, Gail Dexter Lord and Ngaire Blankenberg (Washington, D.C.: AAM Press, 2015), 187–204.

3. This figure is calculated by dividing the population figure of 1.42 billion by the estimated number of museums in China of 5,100 as estimated by the Chinese Museums Association.

4. In the United Kingdom, there are 2,500 museums according to the UK Museums Association ("FAQs," Museums Association, accessed August 20, 2018, https://www.museumsassoci ation.org/about/frequently-asked-questions): "'How many museums are there in the UK?' It is estimated that there are about 2,500 museums in the UK, depending on what you include. Over 1,800 museums have been accredited. Registration under the Accreditation Scheme indicates that a museum has achieved a nationally approved standard in management, collections care and delivery of information and visitor services."

5. In the United States, there are 35,144 museums, according to the IMLS. "More than double the agency's working estimate of 17,500 from the 1990s" (Giuliana Bullard, "Government Doubles Official Estimate: There Are 35,000 Active Museums in the U.S.," last modified May 19, 2014, https://www.imls.gov/ news-events/news-releases/government-doubles-official-esti mate-there-are-35000-active-museums-us).

Chapter 2

1. The International Council of Museums comprises 30,000 members in 137 countries (membership is noncompulsory, so we know this figure is not comprehensive). *The Museums of the World 2017* by De Gruyter Saur lists a total of 55,000 in 202 countries. Guido Guerzoni raises this estimate to 80,000 (Guido Guerzoni, "The Museum Building Boom," in *Cities, Museums and Soft Power*, Gail Dexter Lord and Ngaire Blankenberg [Washington, D.C.: AAM Press, 2015], 187–204).

2. In the United States there are 35,144 museums, according to the IMLS. "More than double the agency's working estimate of 17,500 from the 1990s" (Giuliana Bullard, "Government Doubles Official Estimate: There Are 35,000 Active Museums in the U.S.," last modified May 19, 2014, https://www.imls.gov/ news-events/news-releases/government-doubles-official-esti mate-there-are-35000-active-museums-us).

3. This figure is calculated by dividing the population figure of 1.42 billion by the estimated number of museums in China of 5,100, as estimated by the Chinese Museums Association.

4. "The World Factbook," Central Intelligence Agency, accessed August 30, 2018, https://www.cia.gov/library/publications/ the-world-factbook/fields/2018.html.

5. Barry Lord in his book *Art & Energy: How Culture Changes* (Washington, D.C.: AAM Press, 2014) explains the impact on culture that the oil industry had from the late 1960s. Now it is time to study the impact of the global urban real estate industry on culture.

6. Beatriz Plaza, "The Return on Investment of the Guggenheim Museum Bilbao," *International Journal of Urban and Regional Research* 30, no. 2 (2006): 452–67.

7. International tourist arrivals grew at an average rate of approximately 5 percent over the last decade worldwide, with 7 percent for Asia for the same period. Cultural tourism accounts for 40 percent of world tourism revenues (UNTWO World Tourism Organization, *UNWTO Tourism Highlights 2018 Edition,* accessed August 2018, https://www.e-unwto.org/doi/ pdf/10.18111/9789284419876).

8. Georgina Adam, *Dark Side of the Boom: The Excesses of the Art Market in the 21st Century* (London: Lund Humphries, 2018).

9. Here the private sector refers to philanthropists, corporations, and private nonprofit cultural entities. They often are working with public bodies such as cities and independent urban regeneration agencies.

10. Museum of Old and New Art, "Introduction," accessed August 2018, https://mona.net.au/museum/introduction.

11. Robert Burton Ekelund, John D. Jackson, and Robert D. Tollison, *The Economics of American Art: Issues, Artists, and Market Institutions* (New York: Oxford University Press, 2017), 243.

12. *The Private Art Museum Report*, Larry's List and AMMA, 2016, last accessed September 19, 2018, https://www.larryslist .com/report/Private percent20Art percent20Museum percent 20Report.pdf.

Chapter 3

1. Wang Hongjun, "The History and Culture of China's Museums and Communities—The World's Oldest Museums and the Origin of Museums," *Chinese Museum* 4, 1994.

2. Richard Vinograd, "Classification, Cannon and Genre," in *A Companion to Chinese Art*, eds. Martin J. Powers and Katherine R. Tsiang (Chichester: Wiley and Sons, 2016), 268.

3. Ibid., 261.

4. Marzia Varutti, *Museums in China: The Politics of Representation after Mao* (Woodbridge, UK: The Boydell Press, 2014), 2.

5. Fengting Zhao, "Rethinking the Early Modern Museum in China: In the Context of the Contemporary Museum Boom," Ph.D. dissertation, University of Arizona, August 2016.

6. Marzia Varutti, *Museums in China: The Politics of Representation after Mao*, 26.

7. Fengting Zhao, "Rethinking the Early Modern Museum in China," 8.

8. Ibid.

9. Marzia Varutti, *Museums in China: The Politics of Representation after Mao*, 26.

10. Ibid.

11. Richard Vinograd, "Classification, Cannon and Genre," 268.

12. Marzia Varutti, *Museums in China: The Politics of Representation after Mao*, 27.

13. "The Transition from Palace to Museum: The Palace Museum's Prehistory in the Republican Years," *China Heritage Newsletter* 4 (December 2005), accessed August 22, 2018, http://www .chinaheritagequarterly.org/features.php?searchterm=004_ palacemuseumprehistory.inc&issue=004.

14. Ibid.

15. Ibid.

16. Fengting Zhao, "Rethinking the Early Modern Museum in China."

17. "The Transition from Palace to Museum: The Palace Museum's Prehistory in the Republican Years."

Chapter 4

1. These guidelines were called the "Trial Guidelines for the Preservation of Museum Collections and the Selection Criteria of First-Class Collections."

Chapter 5

1. A. Desvallées and F. Mairesse, *Key Concepts of Museology* (Paris: Armand Colin, 2010), 50.

2. Ministry of Agriculture (China), "China's No. 1 Central Document 2016—Ministry of Agriculture of the People's Republic of China," 2016, accessed September 17, 2017, http://english.agri .gov.cn/news/dqnf/201601/t20160128164966.htm.

3. S. Zheng and D. Wang, "Research on Mode of Wuzhen Tourism Development," *Areal Research and Development* 5 (2012): 18.

4. T. Blumenfield and H. Silverman (eds.), *Cultural Heritage Politics in China* (New York: Springer, 2013). Available at http:// link.springer.com/10.1007/978-1-4614-6874-5 (accessed July 27, 2016).

5. National Cultural Heritage Administration (China), 2015c, *Decision of the Standing Committee of the National People's Congress on Amending the Cultural Relics Protection Law of the People's Republic of China (2015)* 全 国人大常委会关于修改《中华人民 共和国文物保护法》 的决定*(2015)*. Available at http://www .pkulaw. cn/fulltext_form.aspx?Gid=247411 (accessed May 25, 2016).

6. Wenbozaixian, 2017, *Ruhe tuidong feiguoyou bowuguan fazhan? Guojia wenwuju gei yijian le* 如何推动非国有博物馆发展？国家 文物局给意见了 [How to promote the development of private museums? An idea from NCHA]. Available at https://mp.weixin .qq.com/s/hBkkuABsnvGpHSoGsYuA (accessed July 17, 2017).

7. Su, J. "国家文物局: 2017 年让文物自己讲故事 [Let the Cultural Relics Tell Their Stories]," China.org.cn (accessed August 27, 2018, http://guoqing.china.com.cn/2017-02/09/ content_40253388.htm)

8. K. Wang, "Xi Says Protecting Relics a Priority," *China Daily*, April 13, 2016, accessed August 27, 2018, http://www.china daily.com.cn/china/2016-04/13/content_24490576.htm.

9. A government-organized nongovernmental organization (GONGO) is an organization that is set up or sponsored by a government, in order to preserve state power, further its political interests, and mimic the civic groups and civil society at home or promote international or geopolitical interests abroad.

10. Chinese Museums Association Exhibition Exchange Platform, 2016.

11. The "One Belt, One Road" (or OBOR), in Chinese, is referred to as 一带一路, *yi dai yi lu*. More recently, Chinese authorities have adopted the wording "Belt and Road Initiative" in English.

12. J. D. Sidaway and C. Y. Woon, "Chinese Narratives on 'One Belt, One Road' (一带一路) in Geopolitical and Imperial Contexts," *Professional Geographer* 69, no. 4 (2017): 1–13.

13. A "government-organized nongovernmental organization" (GONGO) is an organization that is set up or sponsored by a government in order to preserve state power, further its political interests, and mimic the civic groups and civil society at home, or promote its international or geopolitical interests abroad (see also Naim 2009).

14. L. von Falkenhausen, "Antiquarianism in East Asia: A Preliminary Overview," *World Antiquarianism: Comparative Perspectives* (Los Angeles: Getty Research Institute, 2014).

15. T. Bennett, *The Birth of the Museum: History, Theory, Politics* (London: Routledge, 1995).

16. S. Bollo, *Enshrining Neolithic Pottery? Narratives of the Prehistoric Past in Contemporary Museums in China*, Ph.D. thesis, University of Zurich, 2016.

17. L. von Falkenhausen, "Antiquarianism in East Asia: A Preliminary Overview," *World Antiquarianism: Comparative Perspectives* (Los Angeles: Getty Research Institute, 2014).

18. S. Bollo, *Enshrining Neolithic Pottery? Narratives of the Prehistoric Past in Contemporary Museums in China*, Ph.D. thesis, University of Zurich, 2016.

19. J. A. Flath, "Managing Historical Capital in Shandong: Museum, Monument, and Memory in Provincial China," *Public Historian* 24, no. 2 (2002): 41–59.

20. C. Gray, *The Politics of Museums* (London: Palgrave Macmillan, 2015). Available at http://www.palgraveconnect.com/doifinder/10.1057/9781137493415 (accessed May 9, 2016).

21. M. Falser and M. Juneja (eds.), *Archaeologizing Heritage? Transcultural Entanglements between Local Social Practices and Global Virtual Realities* (Berlin: Springer, 2015).

22. Z.-X. Liang and J.-G. Bao, "Tourism Gentrification in Shenzhen, China: Causes and Socio-Spatial Consequences," *Tourism Geographies* 17, no. 3 (2015): 461–81.

23. J. Leibold, "Filling in the Nation: The Spatial Trajectory of Prehistoric Archaeology in Twentieth-Century China," in B. Molough and P. G. Zarrow (eds.), *Transforming History: The Making of a Modern Academic Discipline in Twentieth-Century China* (Hong Kong: Chinese University Press, 2012), 333–71.

24. J. Johnson and Z. A. Florence, "The Museumification of China," *LEAP* 18 (2013), accessed August 27, 2018, http://leapleapleap.com/2013/05/the-museumification-of-china/.

Chapter 10

1. He Jintang, "Modern Architecture: Concept, Theory, and Cultivation," *Southern Architecture* 1 (2008): 6–11.

2. Fu Wei, "The Ontology of Architectural Creation," *Urbanism and Architecture* 9 (2008): 18.

3. Chen Changyong and Xiao Dawei, "Using Lingnan as the Starting Point to Analyse New Trends in Domestic Architectural Practice," *Architecture Journal* 2 (2010): 68.

4. Feng Jiang, *Returning Home: From Xia Changshi to He Jintang—A Journey through the Evolution of Architecture* 1 (2018): 24.

Chapter 11

1. Interview with Pan Siming conducted at Times Museum by the author, August 2017, as part of the China Residencies Project.

2. "HB STATION: A Case Study of Alternative Art Education in China," Asia Art Archive in America, July 10, 2014, accessed June 25, 2018, http://www.aaa-a.org/programs/hb-station-a-case-study-of-alternative-art-education-in-china/.

3. Rebecca Catching, "V4 Art Museum in Chengdu: Beyond the Edifice and the Artifice," *Ran Dian*, August 4, 2017, accessed June 19, 2018, http://www.randian-online.com/np_review/a4-beyond-the-edifice-and-the-artifice/.

4. Rebecca Catching, interview conducted with Karen Smith in June 2018.

5. Lisa Movius, "Chengdu MoCA Quashes Rumors of Demise, but Its Problems Are Endemic to Art Museums," *Art Newspaper*, August 8, 2018, accessed August 27, 2018, https://www.theartnewspaper.com/news/business-as-usual-at-chengdu-moca-but-for-how-long?utm_source=daily_august8_2018&utm_medium=email&utm_campaign=email_daily&utm_source=The+Art+Newspaper+Newsletters&utm_campaign=10593c25eb-EMAIL_CAMPAIGN_2018_08_03_07_59&utm_medium=email&utm_term=0_c459f924d0-10593c25eb-43581061.

6. Rebecca Catching, "Private Museums and the Curatorial Brain Drain," *Ran Dian* 2 (Winter 2015–2016), accessed August 27, 2018, http://www.randian-online.com/np_feature/private-museums-and-the-curatorial-brain-drain/.

Chapter 12

1. Tracy L-D Liu, *Museums in China: Power, Politics and Identities* (New York: Routledge, 2014), 74.

2. Ibid., 69.

3. Qin Shao, *Culturing Modernity: The Nantong Model, 1890-1930* (Redwood City, CA: Stanford University Press, 2003), 148.

Chapter 13

1. Zhang Ru, "The Chinese Experience: Sino-American Arts Exchange 1972-1986," *Journal of the Hong Kong Branch of the Royal Asiatic Society* 31 (1991): 65, accessed August 19, 2018, http://www.jstor.org/stable/23891028.

2. Rebecca Catching, "Spheres of Influence: Western Art in China and the Vehicles, Actors and the Motives Which Brought It Here," *Ran Dian*, March 3, 2009, accessed August 19, 2018, http://www.randian-online.com/np_feature/spheres-of-influence/.

3. Ibid.

4. NCHA is an influential government body underneath the Ministry of Culture, which governs both museums and cultural heritage sites.

5. Zhang, "The Chinese Experience."

6. Ibid.

7. Paul Richard, "China's Timeless Treasures," *Washington Post*, September 17, 1999, accessed August 19, 2018, https://www.washingtonpost.com/archive/lifestyle/1999/09/17/chinas-timeless-treasures/d7d8cdb9-6837-4c8f-bac2-39195c0ec18d/?utm_term=.4063bf1b5b6e.

8. Craig Smith, "With Fanfare and a Grand Parade, Paris Celebrates France's Ties to China," *New York Times*, January 25, 2004, accessed August 18, 2018, https://www.nytimes.com/2004/01/25/world/with-fanfare-and-a-grand-parade-paris-celebrates-france-s-ties-to-china.html.

9. Holland Cotter, "Art Review; Tricky Mirror of Chinese Power," *New York Times*, February 6, 1998, accessed August 28, 2018, https://www.nytimes.com/1998/02/06/arts/art-review-tricky-mirror-of-chinese-power.html.

Chapter 15

1. You will find several comprehensive overviews of history of the development of Chinese museums in part 1 of this book.

2. "Shanxi Museum," The Best in Heritage, accessed August 2, 2018, http://presentations.thebestinheritage.com/2014/Shanxi%20Museum.

3. "Challenging the Stereotypes of Management," The Best in Heritage, conference publication (Zagreb, 2014).

4. Juan Zhuang, "Beijing 2008: Volunteerism in Chinese Culture and Its Olympic Interpretation and Influence," *International Journal of the History of Sport* 27, no. 16–18 (2010): 2488, 2850.

5. "Suzhou Museum," The Best in Heritage, accessed August 2, 2018, http://presentations.thebestinheritage.com/2014/Suzhou%20Museum.

6. Scott D. Livingston, "Assessing China's Plan to Build Internet Power," Chinafile.com, January 7, 2016, accessed August 3, 2018, http://www.chinafile.com/reporting-opinion/media/assessing-chinas-plan-build-internet-power.

7. "Guangdong Museum," The Best in Heritage, accessed August 2, 2018, http://presentations.thebestinheritage.com/2017/guangdong-museum.

8. straitstimes.com, "19th Party Congress: Xi Jinping Seeks to Turn China into a Nation of Innovators," October 8, 2017, accessed August 2, 2018, https://www.straitstimes.com/asia/east-asia/19th-party-congress-xi-jinping-calls-for-turning-china-into-nation-of-innovators.

9. "Nanjing Museum," The Best in Heritage, accessed August 2, 2018, http://presentations.thebestinheritage.com/2015/Nanjing-Museum.

10. Wang Qizhi, "Nanjing Museum a Palace of Culture and Space and Leisure," The Best in Heritage, accessed August 31, 2018, http://presentations.thebestinheritage.com/2015/Nanjing-Museum.

11. Nanjing was once the capital of the Liao dynasty.

12. Most Innovative Museums Award 2015.

13. "Jianchuan Museum Cluster: China's Largest Private Museum Project," The Best in Heritage, conference publication (Zagreb, 2016).

14. Globaltimes.com, accessed August 2, 2018, http://www.globaltimes.cn/content/1083347.html.

15. "Ministry of Culture and Tourism Inaugurated," Chinadaily.com, last updated April 4, 2018, accessed August 2, 2018, http://www.chinadaily.com.cn/a/201804/08/WS5ac98f72a3105cdcf6516b09.html.

Chapter 16

1. Given the lack of an established written system at the time, the only evidence available on the Xia dynasty is archaeological; therefore, the Three Sovereigns and Five Emperors could only be proto-mythological, which puts them in a netherworld of factuality.

Chapter 18

1. Wang Kaihao, "Palace Museum Limits Those Viewing Famous Painting," *China Daily*, September 25, 2017, accessed August

13, 2018, http://www.chinadaily.com.cn/culture/2017-09/25/content_32445978.htm.

Chapter 19

1. Carol Vogel, "Stuff That Defines Us," *New York Times*, October 28, 2011, accessed August 25, 2018, https://www.nytimes.com/2011/10/30/arts/design/history-of-the-world-in-100-objects-from-british-museum.html.

2. "Ranked Top Ten Most Popular Shows in the World for Their Categories," March 28, 2018, accessed August 25, 2018, *Art Newspaper*, https://www.theartnewspaper.com/feature/top-10-exhibition-and-museum-visitor-figures-2017.

3. Li Yan, "Museums Join Online Marketplace," ECNS, August 9, 2018, accessed August 28, 2018, http://www.ecns.cn/business/2018-08-09/detail-ifywwxaw2290949.shtml.

Chapter 20

1. Davina M. DesRoches, "The Marketized Museum: New Museology in a Corporatized World," *Political Economy of Communication* 3, no. 1 (2015).

2. Ibid.

3. The "One Belt, One Road" initiative announced in 2013 aims for stronger regional economic cooperation between China, Central Asia, Africa, Oceania, and other Asian nations. It has been compared by some pundits to Manifest Destiny or the Monroe Doctrine, and it seems to imply that China should take a greater role in world affairs.

4. "IOT Construction Technology Innovation Alliance in the Field of Cultural Relics Conservation: Smart Museum Case (first series)," *Cultural Relics Press*, November 2017: 7.

Chapter 21

1. These museums include the Chongqing Natural History Museum, Zhejiang Natural History Museum, Shaanxi Natural History Museum, Guangxi Natural History Museum, and Jilin (Northeast Normal University) Natural History Museum.

Chapter 22

1. Holland Cotter, "China's Legacy: Let a Million Museums Bloom," *New York Times,* July 4, 2008, accessed August 16, 2018, https://www.nytimes.com/2008/07/04/arts/design/04museums.html.

2. The literati were a class of scholars, artists, sages, poets, calligraphers, and men of letters.

3. Note, our translation of 文创中国 the company does not appear to have an English name.

Conclusion

1. A megacity is defined as an urban area with more than ten million people. A majority of them are in Asia as of 2018.

2. "Overview of Verbier Art Talks and Conclusions on the 2017 Verbier Art Summit by writer and art critic John Slyce," London, February 15, 2017, http://researchonline.rca.ac.uk/1728/22/Keynote%20speakers%20and%20conclusions%202017%20Summit.pdf.

3. Barry Lord, Gail Dexter Lord, and Lindsay Martin, *Manual of Museum Planning: Sustainable Space, Facilities and Operations*, 3rd ed. (Lanham, MD: AltaMira Press, 2012).

4. Gina Evans, Cuts Survey 2013, October 2013, http://www.museumsassociation.org/download?id=1019920.

BIBLIOGRAPHY

Adam, Georgina. *Dark Side of the Boom: The Excesses of the Art Market in the 21st Century*. London: Lund Humphries, 2018.

Art Newspaper, The. "Ranked Top Ten Most Popular Shows in the World for Their Categories," March 28, 2018. Accessed August 25, 2018. https://www.theartnewspaper.com/feature/top-10-exhibition-and-museum-visitor-figures-2017.

Asia Art Archive in America. "HB STATION: A Case Study of Alternative Art Education in China," July 10, 2014. Accessed June 25, 2018. http://www.aaa-a.org/programs/hb-station-a-case-study-of-alternative-art-education-in-china/.

Barboza, David. "Forging an Art Market in China." *New York Times*, October 23, 2018. Accessed September 12, 2018. http://www.nytimes.com/projects/2013/china-art-fraud/index.html.

Bennett, T. *The Birth of the Museum: History, Theory, Politics*. London: Routledge, 1995.

Best in Heritage, The. "Challenging the Stereotypes of Management." Conference publication, Zagreb, 2014.

———. "Guangdong Museum." Accessed August 2, 2018. http://presentations.thebestinheritage.com/2017/guangdong-museum.

———. "Jianchuan Museum Cluster: China's Largest Private Museum Project." Conference publication, Zagreb, 2016.

———. "Nanjing Museum." Accessed August 2, 2018. http://presentations.thebestinheritage.com/2015/Nanjing-Museum.

———. "Shanxi Museum." Accessed August 2, 2018. http://presentations.thebestinheritage.com/2014/Shanxi%20Museum.

———. "Suzhou Museum." Accessed August 2, 2018. http://presentations.thebestinheritage.com/2014/Suzhou%20Museum.

Blumenfield, T., and H. Silverman (eds). *Cultural Heritage Politics in China*. New York: Springer, 2013. http://link.springer.com/10.1007/978-1-4614-6874-5.

Bollo, S. *Enshrining Neolithic Pottery? Narratives of the Prehistoric Past in Contemporary Museums in China*. Ph.D. thesis, University of Zurich, 2016.

British Council China, The. "Research Report for Museum Professional Development Skills and Higher Education Needs in China," 2016.

Bullard, Giuliana. "Government Doubles Official Estimate: There Are 35,000 Active Museums in the U.S." Last modified May 19, 2014. https://www.imls.gov/news-events/news-releases/government-doubles-official-estimate-there-are-35000-active-museums-us.

Burton Ekelund, Robert, John D. Jackson, and Robert D. Tollison. *The Economics of American Art: Issues, Artists, and Market Institutions*. New York: Oxford University Press, 2017.

Catching, Rebecca. "Spheres of Influence: Western Art in China and the Vehicles, Actors and the Motives Which Brought It Here." *Ran Dian*, March 3, 2009. Accessed August 19, 2018. http://www.randian-online.com/np_feature/spheres-of-influence/.

———. "V4 Art Museum in Chengdu: Beyond the Edifice and the Artifice." *Ran Dian*, August 4, 2017. Accessed June 19, 2018. http://www.randian-online.com/np_review/a4-beyond-the-edifice-and-the-artifice/.

———. "Private Museums and the Curatorial Brain Drain." *Ran Dian* 2 (Winter 2015–2016). Accessed August 27,

2018. http://www.randian-online.com/np_feature/private-museums-and-the-curatorial-brain-drain/.

Central Intelligence Agency. "The World Factbook." Accessed August 30, 2018. https://www.cia.gov/library/publications/the-world-factbook/fields/2018.html.

Changyong, Chen, and Xiao Dawei. "Using Lingnan as the Starting Point to Analyse New Trends in Domestic Architectural Practice." *Architecture Journal* 2 (2010).

China Heritage Newsletter. "The Transition from Palace to Museum: The Palace Museum's Prehistory in the Republican Years," 4 (December 2005). Accessed August 22, 2018. http://www.chinaheritagequarterly.org/features.php?searchterm=004_palacemuseumprehistory.inc&issue=004.

Chinadaily.com. "Ministry of Culture and Tourism Inaugurated." Last updated April 4, 2018. Accessed August 2, 2018. http://www.chinadaily.com.cn/a/201804/08/WS5ac98f72a3105cdcf6516b09.html.

Cotter, Holland. "Art Review; Tricky Mirror of Chinese Power." *New York Times*, February 6, 1998. Accessed August 28, 2018. https://www.nytimes.com/1998/02/06/arts/art-review-tricky-mirror-of-chinese-power.html.

———. "China's Legacy: Let a Million Museums Bloom." *New York Times*, July 4, 2008. Accessed August 16, 2018. https://www.nytimes.com/2008/07/04/arts/design/04museums.html.

Cultural Relics Press. "IOT Construction Technology Innovation Alliance in the Field of Cultural Relics Conservation: Smart Museum Case (first series)." November 2017.

De Gruyter Saur. *The Museums of the World 2017*. Berlin, Boston: De Gruyter Saur, 2017.

DesRoches, Davina M. "The Marketized Museum: New Museology in a Corporatized World." *Political Economy of Communication* 3, no. 1 (2015).

Falkenhausen, L. von. "Antiquarianism in East Asia: A Preliminary Overview." In *World Antiquarianism: Comparative Perspectives*. Los Angeles: Getty Research Institute, 2014.

Falser, M., and M. Juneja (eds). *Archaeologizing Heritage? Transcultural Entanglements between Local Social Practices and Global Virtual Realities*. Berlin: Springer, 2015.

Flath, J. A. "Managing Historical Capital in Shandong: Museum, Monument, and Memory in Provincial China." *Public Historian* 24, no. 2 (2002): 41–59.

Globaltimes.com. Accessed August 2, 2018. http://www.globaltimes.cn/content/1083347.html.

Guerzoni, Guido. "The Museum Building Boom" In *Cities, Museums and Soft Power*, Gail Dexter Lord and Ngaire Blankenberg, 187–204. Washington, DC: AAM Press, 2015.

Hossaini, Ali, and Ngaire Blankenberg. *Manual of Digital Museum Planning*. Lanham, MD: Rowman & Littlefield, 2017.

Hyang Tingting. "The History and Culture of China's Museums and Communities—The World's Oldest Museums and the Origin of Museums." *Chinese Museum* 4 (1994).

Jiang, Feng. *Returning Home: From Xia Changshi to He Jintang—A Journey through the Evolution of Architecture* 1 (2018).

Jintang, He. "Modern Architecture: Concept, Theory, and Cultivation." *Southern Architecture* 1 (2008): 6–11.

Johnson, J., and Z. A. Florence. "The Museumification of China." *LEAP* 18 (2013). Accessed August 27, 2018. http://leapleapleap.com/2013/05/the-museumification-of-china/.

Kaihao, Wang. "Palace Museum Limits Those Viewing Famous Painting." *China Daily*, September 25, 2017. Accessed August 13, 2018. http://www.chinadaily.com.cn/culture/2017-09/25/content_32445978.htm.

Kim, Keun Yong. "Multiculturalism and Museums in China." *University of Michigan, Working Papers in Museum Studies* 7 (2011). Accessed August 2018. https://pdfs.semanticscholar.org/a27d/7c2dbab18d805d51dff4b9cd1a3baba2c82f.pdf.

King, Brad, and Barry Lord. *The Manual of Museum Learning*. Lanham, MD: Rowman & Littlefield, 2016.

Larry's List and AMMA. *The Private Art Museum Report*, 2016. Accessed September 19, 2018. https://www.larryslist.com/report/Privatepercent20Artpercent20Museum percent20Report.pdf.

Lawrence, Elizabeth. "Review Article: Museum Studies, Area Studies and Museums in China." *Museums and Society* 14, no. 1 (March 2016): 220–23.

Liang, Z.-X., and J.-G Bao. "Tourism Gentrification in Shenzhen, China: Causes and Socio-spatial Consequences." *Tourism Geographies* 17, no. 3 (2015): 461–81.

Liu, Tracy L-D. *Museums in China: Power, Politics and Identities*. New York: Routledge, 2014.

Livingston, Scott D. "Assessing China's Plan to Build Internet Power." Chinafile.com, January 7, 2016. Accessed August 3, 2018. http://www.chinafile.com/reporting-opinion/media/assessing-chinas-plan-build-internet-power.

Lord, Barry. *Art & Energy: How Culture Changes.* Washington, DC: Rowman & Littlefield Publishers/American Alliance of Museums, 2014.

Lord, Barry, and Gail Dexter Lord. *Artists, Patrons and the Public: Why Culture Changes.* Lanham, MD: AltaMira Press, 2010.

Lord, Barry, and Maria Piacente. *Manual of Museum Exhibitions.* Lanham, MD: Rowman & Littlefield, 2014.

Lord, Barry, Gail Dexter Lord, and Lindsay Martin. *Manual of Museum Planning: Sustainable Space, Facilities and Operations*, 3rd ed. Lanham, MD: AltaMira Press, 2012.

Lord, Gail Dexter, and Barry Lord. *The Manual of Museum Management*, 2nd ed. Lanham, MD: AltaMira Press, 2009.

Lord, Gail Dexter, and Ngaire Blankenberg. *Cities, Museums and Soft Power.* Washington, D.C.: Rowman & Littlefield Publishers/American Alliance of Museums, 2015.

Lord, Gail Dexter, and Kate Markert. *Manual of Strategic Planning for Cultural Organizations: A Guide for Museums, Science Centers, Gardens, Zoos, Heritage Sites, Libraries, and Performing Arts Centers.* Lanham, MD: Rowman & Littlefield, 2017.

Ministry of Agriculture (China). "China's No. 1 Central Document 2016—Ministry of Agriculture of the People's Republic of China," 2016. Accessed September 17, 2017. http://english.agri.gov.cn/news/dqnf/201601/t20160128164966.htm.

Movius, Lisa. "Chengdu MoCA Quashes Rumors of Demise, but Its Problems Are Endemic to Art Museums." *Art Newspaper*, August 8, 2018. Accessed August 27, 2018. https://www.theartnewspaper.com/news/business-as-usual-at-chengdu-moca-but-for-how-long?utm_source=daily_august8_2018&utm_medium=email&utm_campaign=email_daily&utm_source=The+Art+Newspaper+Newsletters&utm_campaign=10593c25eb-EMAIL_CAMPAIGN_2018_08_03_07_59&utm_medium=email&utm_term=0_c459f924d0-10593c25eb-43581061.

Museum of Old and New Art. "Introduction." Accessed August 2018. https://mona.net.au/museum/introduction.

Museums Association. "FAQs." Accessed August 20, 2018. https://www.museumsassociation.org/about/frequently-asked-questions.

Plaza, Beatriz. "The Return on Investment of the Guggenheim Museum Bilbao." *International Journal of Urban and Regional Research* 30, no. 2 (2006): 452–67.

Richard, Paul. "China's Timeless Treasures." *Washington Post*, September 17, 1999. Accessed August 19, 2018. https://www.washingtonpost.com/archive/lifestyle/1999/09/17/chinas-timeless-treasures/d7d8cdb9-6837-4c8f-bac2-39195c0ec18d/?utm_term=.4063bf1b5b6e.

Ru, Zhang. "The Chinese Experience: Sino-American Arts Exchange 1972-1986." *Journal of the Hong Kong Branch of the Royal Asiatic Society* 31 (1991): 65. Accessed August 19, 2018. http://www.jstor.org/stable/23891028.

Shao, Qin. *Culturing Modernity: The Nantong Model, 1890-1930.* Redwood City, CA: Stanford University Press, 2003.

Sidaway, J. D., and C. Y. Woon. "Chinese Narratives on 'One Belt, One Road' (一带一路) in Geopolitical and Imperial Contexts." *Professional Geographer* 69, no. 4 (2017): 1–13. January 7, 2016. Accessed August 3, 2018.

Si Si. "A Report on Beijing's Cultural Creative Industries Media Clusters." *Global Media and China* 1, no. 4 (2016).

Smith, Craig. "With Fanfare and a Grand Parade, Paris Celebrates France's Ties to China." *New York Times*, January 25, 2004. Accessed August 18, 2018. https://www.nytimes.com/2004/01/25/world/with-fanfare-and-a-grand-parade-paris-celebrates-france-s-ties-to-china.html.

straitstimes.com. "19th Party Congress: Xi Jinping Seeks to Turn China into a Nation of Innovators." October 8, 2017. Accessed August 2, 2018. https://www.straitstimes.com/asia/east-asia/19th-party-congress-xi-jinping-calls-for-turning-china-into-nation-of-innovators.

Su, J. "国家文物局: 2017 年让文物自己讲故事, [Let the Cultural Relics Tell Their Stories]," China.org.cn. Accessed August 27, 2018. www.guo http://guoqing.china.com.cn/2017-02/09/content_40253388.htm.

UNTWO World Tourism Organization. *UNWTO Tourism Highlights 2018 Edition.* Accessed August 2018. https://www.e-unwto.org/doi/pdf/10.18111/9789284419876.

Varutti, Marzia. *Museums in China: The Politics of Representation after Mao.* Woodbridge, UK: The Boydell Press, 2014.

Vinograd, Richard. "Classification, Cannon and Genre." In *A Companion to Chinese Art*, eds. Martin J. Powers and Katherine R. Tsiang. Chichester: Wiley and Sons, 2016.

Vogel, Carol. "Stuff That Defines Us." *New York Times*, October 28, 2011. Accessed August 25, 2018. https://www.nytimes.com/2011/10/30/arts/design/history-of-the-world-in-100-objects-from-british-museum.html.

Wang, K. "Xi Says Protecting Relics a Priority." *China Daily*. Accessed August 27, 2018. http://www.chinadaily.com.cn/china/2016-04/13/content_24490576.htm.

Wang, Qizhi. "Nanjing Museum a Palace of Culture and Space and Leisure." The Best in Heritage. Accessed August 31, 2018. http://presentations.thebestinheritage.com/2015/Nanjing-Museum.

Wei, Fu. "The Ontology of Architectural Creation." *Urbanism and Architecture* 9 (2008).

Wenbozaixian. 2017. *Ruhe tuidong feiguoyou bowuguan fazhan? Guojia wenwuju gei yijian le* 如何推动非国有博物馆发展？国家文物局给意见了 [How to promote the development of private museums? An idea from NCHA]. Accessed July 17, 2017. https://mp.weixin.qq.com/s/hBkkuABsnvGpHSoGsYuA.

Xuefei Ren, *Urban China* (Cambridge: Polity, 2013).

Yan, Li. "Museums Join Online Marketplace." ECNS, August 8, 2018. Accessed August 28, 2018. http://www.ecns.cn/business/2018-08-09/detail-ifywwxaw2290949.shtml.

Zhao, Fengting. "Rethinking the Early Modern Museum in China: In the Context of the Contemporary Museum Boom." Ph.D. dissertation, University of Arizona, August 2016.

Zhongwei, Qin. "Ma Weidu and His Timeless Collection." *China Daily*, November 21, 2010. Accessed September 11, 2018. http://www.chinadaily.com.cn/china/2010-11/21/content_11583212.htm.

Zhuang, Juan. "Beijing 2008: Volunteerism in Chinese Culture and Its Olympic Interpretation and Influence." *International Journal of the History of Sport* 27, no. 16–18 (2010): 2842–62.

INDEX

ABOUT THE EDITORS AND CONTRIBUTORS

An Laishun holds a Ph.D. in Chinese history and a master's in museology. He is the vice president of the International Council of Museums and vice president and secretary general of the Chinese Museums Association. For 34 years, Dr. An has served the museum sector in various positions at the national, regional, and international levels. Working closely with colleagues around the world, he has concentrated his efforts on increasing regional and international cooperation between museums by contributing to the success of a number of programs and projects, and on internationalizing Chinese museums.

Sofia Bollo has an academic background in Chinese studies. She holds a B.A. in Chinese language and culture from the University of Turin and an M.A. in Chinese studies from the School of Oriental and African Studies in London. She also gained work experience in diverse museum institutions in the United Kingdom and Italy. She obtained her Ph.D. from the University Research Priority Program (URPP) Asia and Europe at the University of Zurich. Her research on museums in China focuses on museological narratives in regard to the country's prehistoric past. Her research aims to explore the uses of the past in the present, through displays of archaeological collections of Neolithic pottery in museums in China.

Rebecca Catching is a contemporary art curator and museum planner who lived and worked in China from 2001 to 2017. She has witnessed firsthand many of the developments in China's museum boom. This includes her curatorial work (Minsheng Museum, OV Gallery, Goethe Institute), editorial work (founder of contemporary art magazine *Ran Dian*), and as program director for the International Creative Economy Leadership Academy of Nottingham University—which offered professional development trainings for Chinese museum professionals. Rebecca has written extensively on the topic of museums for a number of publications exploring interpretation, visitor experience, outreach, and the career mobility of Chinese museum professionals.

Chen Ruijin graduated from Nanjing University with a specialization in archaeology and gained extensive experience as a researcher before taking on the directorship of the Suzhou Museum. He has worked exclusively in the field of museums and culture, and in 2014 he received recognition for his contributions, a special award for young and middle-aged museum professionals from the Jiangsu Provincial Government. His research interests include museum management and artifact appraisal, and he has published a series of influential papers on these subjects.

Duan Yong received a doctorate in history from Peking University with a focus on archaeology and museology. He served as the deputy director of the Palace Museum as well as director of the Museums Department of the National Cultural Heritage Administration. He now is the vice president of Shanghai University. His publications include *Contemporary American Museum*, *Imperial Palace of the Ming and Qing Dynasties*, and *Investigation and Research on Lost Cultural Relics from the Palace of Qing Dynasty*, *Contemporary Chinese Museum*.

Phil Enquist is a consulting partner at Skidmore, Owings & Merrill. He is also an architect and urban designer and led the City Design Practice of SOM for 20 years. Phil has been involved in reurbanization strategies in over 100 cities throughout the world—creating livable and transit-based urban districts in collaboration with many designers, economists, and city officials. Phil has taught urban design at the University of Michigan, Harvard University, and the Illinois Institute of Technology. He currently holds a Governor's Chair position in the State of Tennessee, collaborating with Oak Ridge National Laboratory and the University of Tennessee on the subject of energy and urbanism.

Gao Peng is a contemporary art scholar and director of the Today Art Museum. Gao Peng graduated from the Central Academy of Fine Art (Beijing) and University of the Arts (London). He is responsible for the planning and implementation of more than 100 domestic and foreign contemporary art exhibitions. The Today Art Museum has received five awards from the Ministry of Culture of China from 2014 to 2017. His "Future Museum" online platform involves a series of explorations and experiments that have created new precedents for management practices in domestic art museums. In 2015 he served as the cochair of the Global Outstanding Youth Summit at the World Economic Forum in Davos, receiving the title Global Outstanding Youth-Art Ambassador in 2015.

Guan Qiang is currently deputy administrator of the National Cultural Heritage Administration of China, in charge of the Chinese Museums Association and ICOM China. He has been working in the field of archaeological research, exhibition curating, cultural heritage protection, and museum management over the past 30 years, including extensive experience at China's renowned Palace Museum.

Han Yong graduated from Peking University and has served as the director of both the Beijing Stone Carving Art Museum and the Capital Museum in Beijing. He currently serves as the director of the China Millennium Monument World Art Center and acts as a consultant for the construction of the National South China Sea Museum, the Tibet Museum, and the east hall of the Capital Museum, in Beijing.

He Jingtang, Dean of the College of Architecture, South China University of Technology, and vice president of the Architectural Society of China, professor He Jingtang has been in charge of more than 100 important architecture engineering design projects, which have earned him more than 40 provincial and national awards. He has many years of experience in architecture design, teaching, and research, and developed the architectural theory of Two Concepts (holistic and sustainable approaches) and Three Features (place, culture and time). His masterpieces include the Badminton and Wrestling Gymnasium for the Beijing Olympics, the China Pavilion at the 2010 Shanghai Expo, the Opium War Museum of Naval Warfare, the Mausoleum of the Nanyue King, Metropolitan Square, China Mayors Plaza, SCUT Shaw Building of Humanities, and key buildings at Zhejiang University, Chongqing University, and Jiangnan University.

Javier Jimenez is a museum and cultural planner with project experience in more than 20 countries. Since joining Lord Cultural Resources in 2008, Javier has been involved in consulting projects for renowned institutions, including the Guggenheim Museum Bilbao, the King Abdulaziz Center in Saudi Arabia, the Ayala Museum, the Nanjing Museum, and the V&A Museum in London. Javier collaborates regularly with the academic sector. He is an invited professor at the Masters of Cultural Diplomacy from the Universittá Catolica di Roma and has delivered speeches and training sessions for the Chinese Museums Association, ICOM, CAMOC, and UNESCO.

Gail Lord is one of the world's foremost museum, gallery, and cultural planners. Co-founder and president of Lord Cultural Resources, her clients include the Nanjing Museum, Beijing Association of Science and Technology, the Canadian Museum for Human Rights, the Louvre, Tate Modern, and the Museo Guggenheim Bilbao, just to name a few. She is an art critic, feature writer, frequent commentator, public speaker, and the coauthor of several books, including *Cities, Museums, and Soft Power* and *Manual of Strategic Planning for Cultural Organizations*. Gail is a member of the Order of Canada and an officer of the Order of Arts and Letters in the French Ministry of Culture. In 2016, she was awarded an honorary doctor of letters by McMaster University.

Tim Reeve has been deputy director and chief operating officer of the Victoria and Albert Museum (V&A), the world's leading museum of art, design, and performance, since 2013. Tim takes a strategic and operational overview of all museum activities, as well as directly leading the divisions responsible for the V&A's commercial and digital activities, exhibitions, FuturePlan, finance, and resources, marketing and communications, security, and visitor experience. He also leads the V&A's partnership with China Merchant's Group, which saw the creation of the new V&A Gallery at Design Society in Shenzhen and the new "V&A East" in the Queen Elizabeth Olympic Park, East London, which will see a new research and collections center alongside major new permanent gallery and exhibition spaces, as part of the East Bank cultural and educational legacy.

Doug Saunders is an author and journalist of Canadian and British citizenship. He is the author of the books *Arrival City: The Final Migration and Our Next World* (2011), *The Myth of the Muslim Tide* (2012), and *Maximum Canada* (2017) and is the international-affairs columnist for the Canadian national newspaper the *Globe and Mail*. He served as the paper's London-based European bureau chief for a decade after running the paper's Los Angeles bureau, and has written extensively from East Asia, the Indian Subcontinent, the Middle East, and North Africa. He writes a weekly column devoted to the larger themes and intellectual concepts behind international news and has won the National Newspaper Award, Canada's counterpart to the Pulitzer Prize, on five occasions, as well as the Schelling Prize for Architectural Theory, the Donner Prize, and the National Library of China Wenjin Book Award.

Shan Jixiang graduated from the School of Architecture, Tsinghua University, and received a doctorate in engineering. He is a doctoral supervisor and adjunct professor at a number of universities and colleges, including Peking

University and Tsinghua University. In March 2005, Dr. Shan received the International Leadership Award issued by the American Planning Association (APA). A senior architect and registered city planner, Dr. Shan Jixiang was successively appointed deputy director of Beijing Municipal Administration of City Planning, director of the Beijing Municipal Administration of Cultural Heritage, director of Beijing Municipal Commission of Urban Planning, and administrator of National Cultural Heritage Administration of China. In 2012, he became the director of the Palace Museum. His major publications include *Cultural Heritage: Thoughts and Practice* and *From "Gallery Space" to "Boundless Universe": Contemplating the Museum in a Broader Sense.*

Chen Shen is a senior curator and currently serves as vice president of art and culture at the Royal Ontario Museum. He received his Ph.D. in anthropological archaeology from the University of Toronto in 1997, and his research interests focus on Asian Paleolithic archaeology and human evolution, cultural heritages, and museum studies. Among many publications, Dr. Shen published *Anyang and Sanxingdui: Unveiling the Mysteries of Ancient Chinese Civilizations* (2002) and is the co-editor of *Relevance and Application of Heritage in Contemporary Society* (2018), the "Human Evolution and Peopling of America" section for *Encyclopedia of Global Archaeology* (2014), *Archaeological Study of Lithic Use-Wear Experiments* (2008, in Chinese), and *Stories of Archaeology in Foreign Lands Series* (since 2015, in Chinese).

Tomislav Sola is the founder of the Best in Heritage conference—an annual, global conference featuring award-winning museum, heritage, and conservation projects. After finishing a degree in art history at the University of Zagreb and a course in museology at the Sorbonne in Paris, he completed his Ph.D. in museology at the University of Ljubljana. He has held the post of director of the Museum Documentation Centre in Zagreb and later became involved in ICOM first as national committee chairman and then as a member of EC of ICOM. He has occupied the positions of head of the Department of Information Sciences and chair of museology at the University of Zagreb and regularly teaches at seven different international universities. He was a member of the jury of EMYA and headed the Europa Nostra jury, where he is now a council member. Professor Sola has completed 325 hours of international lectures and published eight books, individual chapters in nine books, and over 250 articles. Although retired from his position at the university, he now continues to consult, write, and lecture internationally.

Song Xiangguang is a professor at the School of Archaeology and Museology at Peking University, a distinguished professor of the graduate school of the Chinese Academy of Social Sciences, and executive director of Chinese Museums Association. He served as a professor of the School of Archaeology and Museology at Peking University, where he was deputy curator of the Arthur M. Sackler Museum of Art and Archaeology. He studied museum science and museum collections management at the Smithsonian Institution in the United States and at University College London. He has published dozens of papers on museum studies, including "Material and Cognition—An Analysis of the Theory and Practice of Contemporary Chinese Museums."

Tian Kai graduated from the department of archaeology of Peking University in 1985 and currently acts as director of the Henan Provincial Bureau of Cultural Relics, executive member of the Security Committee of the International Council of Museums, the State-Council Appointed Expert, an Outstanding Expert of the Ministry of Culture, Research Scientist of Artifacts and Museology. He also acts in the capacity of graduate tutor of Zhengzhou University, Henan University, Minzu University of China, and the University of Science and Technology of China. Mr. Tian has served as president of the Henan Museum and vice president of the Chinese Museums Association, where he specializes in museums management and cultural artifacts research. To date, he has published over 100 papers and academic works.

Wei Jun has been the director of Guangdong Museum since 2012. Under his leadership, the GDM has become an epicenter for art, culture, and natural history, attracting some 1,800,000 annual visitors. Previously, he served as the assistant director of the Guangdong Provincial Institute of Archaeology and deputy director of the Guangdong Cultural Relics Administration. Dr. Wei is a board member of ICOM-ASPAC and the president of Guangdong Provincial Museums Association. Dr. Wei has published over forty academic essays on museum studies, underwater archaeology, and cultural heritage conservation. Wei has curated more than ten exhibitions in recent years, including "Sailing the Seven Seas: Legend of Ming Maritime Trade during the Wanli Era" (2015) and "Historical Imprints of Lingnan" (2014).

Yu Zhang has an M.A. in cultural and media management from the Institut d'Études Politiques de Paris, France, and a B.A. in French literature from the University of International Studies of Shanghai, China. With experience in event management and publishing, she has occupied different roles at the International Council of Museums (ICOM), where she worked as head of the Communications Department between 2013 and 2016. Since 2016, she has worked as a museum consultant, and in 2017 she founded Yu Culture—a Paris-based company that provides consulting to cultural institutions on their China-related projects and partnerships. She regularly lectures on Chinese museums and trends in the Chinese cultural sector. She is now the

Director of Communications and Digital at National Air and Space Museum of France.

Yang Zhigang has been teaching at Fudan University for many years as a professor and a doctoral supervisor. His research interests include Chinese culture and ideology and cultural heritage and museology. He is the dean of the Department of Cultural Heritage and Museology; chief of academic research for the humanities; and dean of the National Institute for Advanced Humanistic Studies. In 2014, Professor Yang became the director of Shanghai Museum and vice president of Chinese Museums Association. *The Study of Chinese Rites* is just one of his many well-regarded publications.

Zhou Ming After graduating from Peking University in 1983, majoring in archaeology, Zhou Ming has taken on an influential role at the National Cultural Heritage Administration of China. His main work concerns research on policies and regulations, international exchange exhibitions, and museums management. He played a key role in many international exchange exhibition projects, including "Chinese Treasures," which toured Japan, the Czech Republic, Hungary, Qatar, Peru, and Saudi Arabia, and other related cultural relics exhibitions in the United Kingdom, including the "Underground Treasures of the Han Dynasty," "Famous Chinese Paintings Exhibition," and the "Ming Dynasty: 50 Years of a Prosperous Imperial Dynasty."

Zhu Pei is dean of Central Academy of Fine Arts, School of Architecture; visiting professor, Harvard University; and adjunct professor, Columbia University, Zhu Pei is one of China's leading architects. He received his master's degree in architecture both from Tsinghua University and UC Berkeley and went on to found Studio Zhu-Pei in Beijing in 2005. Zhu Pei is the recipient of a number of awards, including the Future Project Awards (2017, *Architectural Review*) and the Award of Honor (2015, AIA). In addition, he was named one of "the 5 greatest architects under 50" by the *Huffington Post* in 2011, won the Courvoisier Design Award by *Wallpaper* in 2009, the Design Vanguard Award by *Architectural Record* in 2007, and the Special Merit Award by UIA and UNESCO in 1989. In 2006 and 2007, Zhu Pei was commissioned by the Guggenheim Foundation to design the Guggenheim Art Pavilion in Abu Dhabi. His built works include Digital Beijing, Olympics Control Center (2008), and OCT Design Museum and Minsheng Museum of Modern Art (Beijing, 2015).